# OF LAW IN

# PORTS OF THE WORLD

SHERRY HUTT

Copyright © 2022 by Sherry Hutt

All rights reserved. No part of this book may be reproduced or transmitted in any form or by any means, electronic or mechanical, including photocopying, recording, or by any information storage and retrieval system without the written permission of the author, except where permitted by law.

Bound: ISBN: 978-1-942153-32-0

Epub: ISBN: 978-1-942153-33-7

# TABLE OF CONTENTS

Preface .................................................................................................. 5
Introduction ....................................................................................... 7
Map ................................................................................................... 12
Timeline ............................................................................................ 13
Ports of Law
    Natural/Environmental Law – Orkney & Shetland –
    Stones of Time ............................................................................ 15
    Representative Democratic Government – Norway to Iceland –
    Viking Things .............................................................................. 25
    Domestic Relations – Dublin - Táin bó Cuailnge and The Cattle
    Raid of Cooley ............................................................................. 37
    Intellectual Property/Copyright – Ireland/Scotland– St. Columba
    and the Book of Kells ................................................................. 41
    Non-Belligerents in War – Iona – Bishop Adomnán's Law
    of Innocents ................................................................................. 49
    Civil Code (Political License) – Scotland – Code of Macbeth
    vs Shakespeare's Macbeth ........................................................... 53
    Tax Court – Winchester – Domesday Book & Taxes of
    William I ...................................................................................... 61
    Commercial Code – Lübeck, Warnemünde & Rostock –
    The Hanseatic League ................................................................ 69
    Land Title - Germany - Schwabenspiegel Code of Fiefdoms ......... 77
    Corporate Securities – Amsterdam – The Dutch East
    India Company ........................................................................... 83

Debtors & Bankruptcy – Amsterdam - Tulip Envy
to Tulip Frenzy ................................................................................. 89

Banking & Securities Regulation – Lorient – Banking, John Law
& the French Stockholders............................................................. 95

Contract - Seville – Columbus Brings Suit in Contract.................. 105

Zoning – Spain & Spanish New World – Law of the Indies .......... 119

Banking -Genoa – Financing Columbus & Marco Polo.................. 127

Probate/Custody - Herculaneum – Justice for Justa ....................... 133

Civil Code – Rome – Twelve Tables to Corpus Juris Civilus........... 141

Sports – Constantinople/Istanbul - Nika Riot, Corpus Juris and
Hagia Sophia ................................................................................. 145

Historic Preservation/Repatriation - Egypt & Sudan -
Shabaka's Stone and the Rosetta Stone ......................................... 153

Civic Administration - India and China - Confucius and
the Arthasastra .............................................................................. 169

INDEX ................................................................................................. 177

# PREFACE TO CTH SERIES

Cruise through History is a collection of short stories grouped by sequence of popular cruise itineraries, into fifteen volumes. As stories move from port to port, they randomly move through time. Stories are all true. They introduce travelers to history and culture of a port through a long-ago, or not so long-ago, resident, whose exploits left a castle, palace, or lovely site to explore. Cruise through History of the Law crosses itineraries, traversing the globe, bringing topical stories into one volume/itinerary.

Host characters are chosen for inspiring actions and visible remnants on the landscape. Some names are familiar, presented with depth to their personality. Others will be new friends, too long unrecognized. Stories offer a twist to school-age history of place, putting travels in fascinating context for short-term visitors. Travel is an opportunity for events of life to give rich meaning to facts for which fiction is no rival.

No apology is made for the choice of subjects. They were chosen arbitrarily, on whim of the author, accumulated from past travels, for your enjoyment. Readers share the fun. No attempt is made for political correctness or a chamber of commerce gloss. Knowledge of history teaches us a great deal about ourselves and the human condition, but only if it is honest and fairly told. The quest for "real" draws adults to travel.

Praise is due to historians and scholars who delve into source data to ponder minute details of history. Footnotes give due credit to scholars and remind the reader that stories are true. Editorial sidebars and fun bits are in footnotes. History is a public good. The more it is enjoyed, the more it is valued.

Gaps in facts are not supplemented by fiction. Rather, stories relate the known as a guide to the unknown. Readers draw their own conclusions, daydream through gaps, and enjoy the reason so much popular fiction and movies are drawn from historical facts.

Stories give historical context to sites visited as cruise destinations. In these stories, meet characters who walked the same streets visitors walk today. Go beyond buildings to envision people who built them and lived there.

Stories in Cruise through History itineraries inspire cruise travelers to rise out of deck chairs to investigate a destination with honesty and irreverence, or the potential traveler to rise from the sofa and embark on a Cruise through History. There is no stigma of a school assignment. Earn an "E" for enjoyment.

Itineraries in the Cruise through History series available as books and e-books are:

1. London to Rome
2. Rome to Venice
3. Ports of the Eastern Mediterranean
4. Ports of the Black Sea
5. Ports of Arabia to the Atlantic
6. Ports of the Atlantic Coast of North America, with Cuba and Bermuda
7. Ports of the Pacific Coast of North America, with Hawaii
8. Mexico, Central America, and the Caribbean
9. Ports of South America
10. Ports of the British Isles
11. Ports of the Baltic Sea
12. Ports of the North Sea
13. Ports of Africa, India, and Southeast Asia
14. Ports of the South Pacific - Australia, New Zealand, and Polynesia
15. Ports of the Far East, with Indonesia.

Check out Cruisethroughhistory.com for blogs, CTH Virtual Travel Group events, videos, and release of new books, the CTH World Coloring Book, and pod casts.

# INTRODUCTION

Welcome to a Cruise through History of the Law. In this volume, the cruise itinerary floats to ports of the world for stories illuminating use of law in civil society, to adjudicate rights between people applying agreed upon principles, rather than force. There is no assumption that these stories are the earliest use of principles of law, nor is this volume comprehensive. Stories are chosen as delightful instances, illustrative of early use of legal principles, taught to suffering law students today as twentieth century innovations.[1]

This volume of stories avoids religious laws, such as Talmud, Sharia, or Vatican law. It omits archaic trial by fire, drowning, or combat. Criminal law is not represented here, as crimes have evolved from common law to statutory, as punishments have evolved from banishment and payment in sheep or cows, to incarceration and fines. Novel means found by communities to punish offenders are not always instructive as communities grapple with reflecting their humanity in choices of punishment or rehabilitation.

As these stories illustrate, rights litigated today were adjudicated in sophisticated venues a millennium or two ago, providing instructive precedent. In these stories, lawyers may find creative solutions to vexing cases. Judges may pause prior to authoring a lengthy opinion, as though elucidating a newly discovered treatise, only to find the matter well decided centuries ago. While quoting Macbeth, Columba, or the *Arthasastra* may not change outcomes, it will give

---

[1] Consider William Lloyd Prosser, Dean of Law at Berkeley, when he amassed *Prosser on Torts* in 1941. The Uniform Commercial Code was first published in 1951. The casebook movement began in 1923, with the American Law Institute Restatement of the Law series. E. Allen Farnsworth completed the Restatement of Contracts, 2$^{nd}$ edition in 1981, spawning decades of casebooks on genre of law, including Heritage Resources Law in 1999.

opponents pause and awaken interest of an appreciative jurist. These stories are intended as fun diversions, inspiring travel destinations.

Travel to the core of legal principles impels definition of natural and common law. Natural Law is often equated to moral principles, developed in righteous life, construed as the basis of religious law. In the time span of these stories, religion is a recent concept. The Stones of Time in Orkney, Shetland, and elsewhere in Scotland, reveal a Natural Law in harmony with the environment. Druids held wisdom for survival on the land.

Common Law is a law of precedent, developed over time, and understood as rules of the community. Besides building roads to traverse their known universe, from Constantinople to the border of England and Scotland at Hadrian's wall, Romans were avid recorders of legal precedent. Romans denied coopting Greek law, even as they borrowed from Greeks forms of architecture, poetry, and a pantheon of gods.

Romans were latecomers to Egypt and Sudan, where pharaohs of two dozen dynasties crafted laws written on papyrus and stone. Shabaka, a pharaoh of the little-praised twenty-fifth dynasty of a thrice united Egypt, preserved in stone words of the first dynasty crumbling to bits on papyrus. Shabaka's legacy included first dynasty concepts of constitutional monarchy and twenty-fifth dynasty historic preservation.

A millennium prior to ancient Greek written language, a well-font of Western law, Sanskrit was the language of literate Africa, India, and Asia. Emanating from the subcontinent of India, the *Arthasastra* was written in the $2^{nd}$ century BCE as an authoritative treatise on statecraft, as well as economic and military policy. Wisdom of the *Arthasastra* is timeless instruction, accessible in English.

Before Mount Vesuvius erupted, covering Herculaneum in mud, the beach town was an enclave of vacation homes. Few structures remain. The story of Justice for Justa recalls lengthy litigation in Roman probate court, to secure freedom from a life of servitude for a young woman, pursuing claims to assets in her mother's estate.

Travel to castles in Germany to experience the Schwabenspiegel Code of Fiefdoms. The Code established property rights in ownership and land use.

These concepts survive, although bonds of feudal systems were broken in the renaissance of commerce, entrepreneurship, and freedom of non-royals to amass more wealth than royals in the Law of Lübeck, founding document of the Hanseatic League. The story of the Hanseatic League is told in ports of Lübeck, Warnemünde, and Rostock, Germany.

Christopher Columbus was a young man of Genoa, sailing the Seven Seas for bankers invested in sugar trade across the Old World. Later, the bank financed his third voyage of discovery to the New World, established a gold standard, and set rules for loans and credit. The bank and its concepts stand today in Genoa. Columbus left home to sail for Spain. Once he discovered a New World for the Spanish monarchs, he brought a court case to protect his contractual rights to hereditary title and income from discoveries.

Dock in Lorient, a quiet port today, to walk cobblestone streets of the French East India Company. This story is a cautionary tale of government involvement in securities, investment schemes, and the implosion of a limited liability company that toppled the monarchy. Learn why the word "bank" is not used in France. Then travel to Amsterdam for the story of tulips as securities in bubble-bursting-bankruptcy. Amsterdam is home to the Dutch East India Company, the first shareholder held trade consortium. DEIC was a model for French and British East India and West India companies from 1602 to its demise when Napoleon inspected the books in 1799 and declared it insolvent.

Cruise through History of the Law sails to the British Isles, porting in Dublin for an early domestic relations dispute, recorded in Irish epic poetry, *Táin bó Cuailnge*. In dispute was custody of a prize bull, rescued by a tragic hero. Also in Ireland, home of the Book of Kells, is the first known intellectual property and copyright action, between monks, which escalated to battle. Meanwhile, in Scotland, the much-maligned Macbeth, a much-appreciated monarch, issued a civil code, giving fair treatment to all in his realm. The monastery at Iona, where Macbeth lies in the graveyard, was domain of Bishop Adomnán when he crafted a code for non-combatants in war, a model for the Lieber Code, written for President Abraham Lincoln, decades prior to the Hague Convention.

Sailing to Bergen, Norway and Reykjavik, Iceland follows the course of Vikings preserving democratic government tradition in annual Things. Pause along the fissure of rocky earth in Iceland, where Vikings held law courts and legislative sessions since the tenth century. In Winchester, England the story venue is the tax court of William I, to this day the location of an annual procession of newly admitted barristers.

Cruise to ports of Mexico, Central, and South America, where the zoning decree of Spanish king Philip II in the Law of the Indies is still evident in Spanish colonial towns. Cathedrals anchored main squares of Spanish hill towns along the Pacific coast and throughout South America. Priests, not politicians, were the predominant authority.

As stories float through time and across the globe, they leave travelers and readers with a sense that law is more than a rigorous field of study. Reflecting on application of law in lives lived long ago, is a fun bit of harmless voyeurism. Law texts are compendiums of stories illustrating legal principles. CTH adds in fun. Enjoy your travels!

**CTH**

# DEDICATION

This volume is dedicated to those law professors who tried in vain to instill in me an understanding of law in its Socratic method, my fellow lawyers, and jurists, who added to my practical understanding of the law, hopefully to its highest and best use, and to the appellate judges who ruminated over my successes and failures to accurately portray the law. To all, be relieved that this tome does not profess to be a scholarly work.

In the twenty years since retiring from the bench, I have realized that no matter how far we travel, and how often, we never fully unpack our bags. Our lives are an accumulation of experiences. Fortunate are those who enjoy life, complete with baggage.

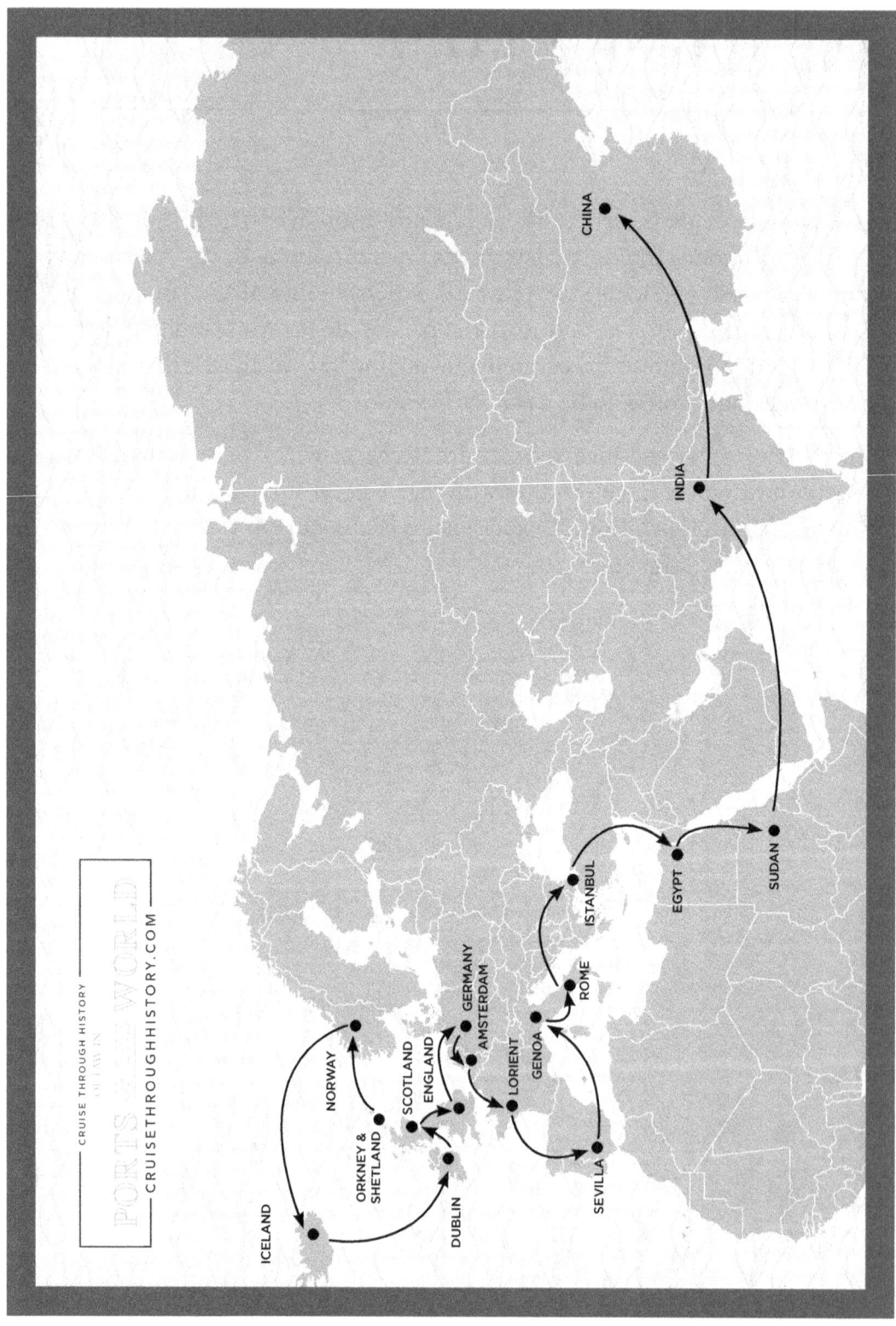

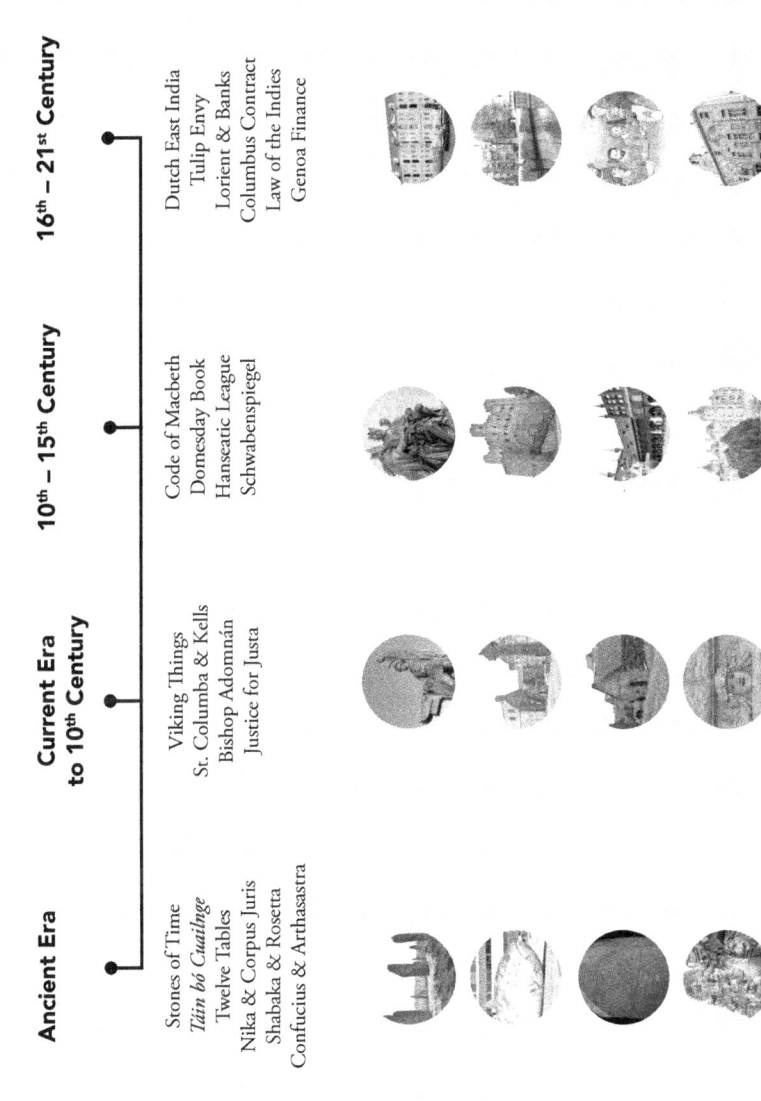

*Clockwise from upper left, Skara Brae Orkney Island, Ring of Brodgar, Newgrange Ireland, and Jarlshof Shetland*

# NATURAL/ENVIRONMENTAL LAW - ORKNEY & SHETLAND ISLANDS

## Stones of Time

When embarking on travels into realms of people, as they began social organizations, well known are pyramids of Egypt. Lesser known are sites older than the pyramids, such as Newgrange in Ireland. Ancient people left a legacy of dwellings, ceremony sites, and passage graves of stone. Over thousands of years, people repurposed stones, plowed fields, and dispersed evidence of early life.

Few places remain where visitors can peer into ancient homes and appreciate life near the sea thousands of years ago. In Skara Brae, in the Orkney Islands and Jarlshof, in the Shetland Islands, storms in the 19th century uncovered dwellings, where archaeological investigation continued into the 20th century, giving insight to lives of islanders five thousand years ago. In the stones are stories.

Windswept and treeless, northern islands of Orkney and Shetland, fifty miles apart, have populations of less than fifty thousand in total today. It is hard to imagine that five thousand years ago these Northern Islands of Great Britain were thriving with population. Preserved in stone are some of the best stone-age settlement sites in all Europe.

Standing Stones of Stenness and Ring of Brodgar on Orkney are reminiscent of stonehenges throughout England. In Skara Brae and Jarlshof are round, stone dwellings in communities of size seen nowhere else in England. They were occupied as communities fishing, farming, and manufacturing trade goods in cooperative settings.

Shetland and Orkney Island groups have similar histories. Human presence is evidenced from 6800 BCE. The Neolithic, that is Stone Age, settlements date from 3100 BCE. Northern Islands passed from Celtic people in final centuries of the ancient era to control by Romans in the current era, looking for the northern-most point of their world, they called Thule. Romans determined Thule was Shetland. In fact, Romans were accurate. The northernmost point of Great Britain is the Shetland Island of Out Stack.

Vikings came to the Northern Islands in the 9th century. Their island homes provided ports in storms while raiders were out *A Viking*, looting monasteries and settlements in England. A large percentage of Northern Islanders have Norse heritage. Place names are Norse and Scottish. In the medieval era of nation-building, Northern Islands passed from the Kalmar Union of Norway, Denmark, and Sweden, to Scotland, then to Britain in 1707.

Ancient stones of Skara Brae and Jarlshof begin the story of Great Britain. Ancient people of the islands were remarkable in their ability to live in harsh environment. At Kirkwall in Orkney and Lerwick in Shetland, history is recent, as the world watches the Northern Islands move toward a future as strategic points in the race for ocean resources.

## A Little History of the Northern Islands: Shetland and Orkney

Travelers may think of the Northern Islands as remote. Six thousand years ago, when humans swarmed across these islands, remote was any group living more than several islands away. Waters were sources of food, protection from hostile groups, and access to friendly islands. Inter-island trade developed naturally. Commonalities suggest contact.

There are seventy islands in the Orkneys, twenty of which have permanent residents today. There are one hundred islands in the Shetlands, sixteen of which are inhabited today. In ancient times, most of the islands supported human existence.

In the absence of wood, Northern Islanders built shelters of stone. Stone has permanence. Settlements grew, in place, over longer periods of time than farming settlements in lower England. There people moved from field to field, and yet had little contact with people a hundred miles away. Northern Island stone shelters were cooperative settlements.

Six thousand years ago, sea levels were much lower. Some islands were connected. There were trees, abundant vegetation, and wildlife. Trees were cleared for farmland as communities grew, four thousand years ago.[2]

Early people of the Northern Islands share similarities in stone tool technology with people of Europe, suggesting the islands were populated from Europe. Neolithic people built stone dwellings and farmed, displacing earlier Mesolithic people, who melded into later groups or succumbed to greater forces. Similar questions of destiny exist for Neolithic people, displaced by Celtic groups, of which Picts of Scotland are most prominent. When Romans arrived in the 1st century, history was documented.

Romans did not stay in the Northern Islands any longer than necessary to hunt for Thule, the northern edge of the world. Then they dropped back to Hadrian's Wall in defense against Picts. Picts caused Romans to abandon their forward position at the Antonine Wall in Scotland in the 150s CE and drop back to Hadrian's Wall.

Collapse of the Roman Empire in the current era,[3] left a void. The power vacuum was filled in England by Saxons and Anglos from Germanic tribes of Europe, and by Norsemen in the Northern Islands. Norse and Scots battled for control of the Northern Islands, as their respective domains became discernable political units of Norway and Scotland. People of the Shetlands and Orkneys were captive to powers battling for control.

---

[2] Caroline Wickham-Jones, Monuments of Orkney, Historic Scotland publication, 2017, pp. 6-7. See also, Caroline Wickham-Jones, Orkney, A Historical Guide, Birlinn Limited, Edinburgh, 2015; and Dr. David Clarke, Skara Brae, Historic Scotland, Edinburgh, 2012, 2016.

[3] Current Era, Common Era, or Christian Era, all CE. The time prior to CE is Before Common Era or BCE.

Viking is a label often used for all Norse peoples expanding their domain in the 9th to 11th centuries. Among Norse, going *a-viking* meant to raid and pillage. There is a distinction between Norse men and women, who ventured beyond Norway, settling and farming in Northern Islands in the 9th century, while kinsmen went *a-viking*. Northern Island settlements were peaceful havens during seasons of farming.[4]

By the 11th century, Dublin was a community of former Vikings, domesticated and politically active. Viking king Canute was the great king of Norway, England, and Denmark. Viking warriors traveled as far as Constantinople as mercenaries of kings. In Britain and Norway, Norse kings were heralded for bringing Christianity to their people.

King Olaf II of Norway came to Shetland Islands and gave people the choice of Christianity or death.[5] Most chose Christianity, at least facially. Some Norse became Christian in 995 under prompting by Olaf I. Picts, the conquered people, had long-standing Christian traditions. Irish monasteries trained missionaries from the 6th century. In the Norse-Christian era, churches of stone appeared on the Northern Island landscape.

The 10th and 11th centuries in the Northern Islands are known as the Earls of Norway era. Earls were leaders of warriors evolved from Viking raiders to protectors of their turf. Magnus Eriendsson was an Earl of Norway, known for piety and peaceful Christian virtue. He jointly ruled Orkney with his cousin Håkon. Their lives are chronicled in 12th century Norse Sagas, one of which is Orkney Saga. Orkney refers generally to Northern Islands.

Followers of Magnus and Håkon were competitive. In Viking fashion, they agreed to meet at a *Thing*, the Viking democratic forum for resolving disputes. It was decided that each earl should bring two ships of warriors in 1116, and battle for prominence on the Orkney Island of Egilsay. Magnus kept to the agreement. Håkon arrived with eight ships of warriors, overwhelming the Magnus group. In the fray, Magnus was captured. He offered to be a prisoner or exiled, as was the custom. Instead, he was hit in the head with an axe.

---

4  Norse Sagas, written in the 11th and 12th centuries, gave detailed accounts of Norse kings, who farmed in season and went raiding in off seasons.
5  Known as St. Olaf in Norway, he lived from 995 to 1030. His successor was King Canute.

Magnus was vigorously mourned by his followers. Miracles were seen near his burial, where crops were notably productive. Magnus was heralded as a saint. Håkon's penance was to erect a church in 1117, at the place where Magnus died. St. Magnus Church was later rebuilt larger. It stands today as an historic monument on Egilsay Island, Orkney.

In 1129, the earldom of Orkney went to the nephew of Magnus, Rögnvald Kolsson. He was sent to Orkney from Norway to build a cathedral to St. Magnus, fit to entomb holy relics of the saint. The result was St. Magnus Cathedral in Kirkwall. St. Magnus was canonized in 1135. Construction of the Kirkwall cathedral began in 1137.

During church construction, battles between Scottish lords and Norse Earls continued. In one battle, Rögnvald was killed. He was recognized as a local Norse saint in 1192, and his relics were placed in the cathedral.[6] Impetus for St. Magnus Cathedral was long thought only a legend of Norse Sagas, until 19th century restoration work on the cathedral exposed a cracked skull. The spirit of St. Magnus remains in the cathedral.[7]

Norse control of Northern Islands ebbed in 1231, when powerful Earl John of Orkney was killed in a pub brawl.[8] Other families of Norse earls married into Scottish noble families. In 1290, hopes of a joinder of Norway, Scotland, and England died with Princess Margaret of Norway, while the child bride was sailing to England to marry Edward Prince of Wales, the son of King Edward I of England. Margaret was the granddaughter and heir to Alexander III, king of Scotland. In 1249, in a treaty, Alexander III conceded the Northern Islands to Norway in exchange for the Hebrides and Isle of Man. His granddaughter was an emissary of peace joining Norway and England.

Finally, the fate of Orkney and Shetland was settled, not on a battlefield, rather by nuptial gift. By the 15th century, Norway was part of the Kalmar Union of Norway, Denmark, and Sweden. Denmark was the dominant power, after deft maneuvers in which royals of the other countries were executed at a dinner

---

[6] Sainthood of Rögnvald is a matter of dispute.
[7] During Protestant Reformation wars in 1614, Kirkwall Castle was leveled. St. Magnus Cathedral remains the oldest example of early medieval era architecture.
[8] Wickham-Jones, Monuments of Orkney, at 18.

party. In 1469, King Christian I of Denmark, head of the Kalmar Union, gave his daughter Margaret in marriage to King James III of Scotland. To secure payment of her dowry, Christian pledged Orkney and Shetland Islands. He defaulted. The Northern Islands were part of Scotland by 1472. Scotland became part of Great Britain in the 1707 Act of Union.

## Stories in Stones of Skara Brae and Jarlshof

While battles occurred around, and sometimes above, stone monuments of Skara Brae and Jarlshof, settlements of Neolithic people lie preserved in sand. Few population centers grew in the Northern Islands, leaving ancient cultures unscathed. In the mid to late 19th century, storms battered northern coasts, ripping sandy banks into the sea.

Storms left exposed stone settlements of amazing structural integrity, over extensive terrain. Fortunately, sites were exposed when Great Britain was experiencing a strong preservation ethic. Archaeology undertaken at Skara Brae in Orkney and Jarlshof in Shetland restored and preserved sites, which are visitor favorites.

A Skara Brae, the site sits against the beach, protected from erosion by a recently constructed sea wall. It is easy to imagine the site much larger almost five thousand years ago, when actively occupied. An undetermined number of homes washed into the sea.

Skara Brae was occupied from 3360 to about 3160 BCE, although earliest occupants did not build the settlement seen today. The more recent settlement began about 2900 BCE. The site sat vacant for two hundred and fifty years, collecting soil and sand deposits, and was then occupied for four hundred years.

The impetus for people leaving and returning to Skara Brae cannot be determined from the archaeological record. There are no other sites on Orkney to which people gravitated. There is no evidence of a major destructive storm, or conquest by warring people.

Skara Brae is remarkable in the number of houses in clusters and the interior furnishings. Houses are all circular, reinforced into soil banks with double rows of stone. Between stone walls was discarded material mixed with sand and soil. Walls provided insulation and held against the wind.

There are deep passageways between houses. Around interior walls are circular side chambers, likely used for storage. The sloping roofs were thatched with grasses.

Each house is identical in interior design. Furniture is of stone. In the center of each house is a stone-lined fire pit. Opposite the entrance, is a two-level, built-in, storage unit. To each side of the large chamber is a stone-lined bed. A circular chamber, larger than others, without beds, was a workshop or communal storage area.

So many, well-carved tools and beads were found in Skara Brae that archaeologists had three scenarios for its purpose. Either Skara Brae was a religious site of high status, to which people brought tributes; or it was a wealthy residential settlement of long stature; or it was a place of craftsmen, from which items were distributed throughout the area.

Clues to settlement life are in the stones. Doorways were small to keep out cold winds. Doors could be secured by bars to bolt a rock door from the inside. People kept out the weather, or sought privacy and security, in the tight village of fifty to one hundred people.

A village of conforming features evidence social organization and cooperation. People farmed and caught wild animals from which leather was used for clothing. There was no evidence of weaving on the site. There was nothing to burn for heat besides grasses and few trees, which were depleted. People had food security. Fuel was scarce.

Also mysterious on Orkney are standing stone henges in the Ring of Brodgar, ten miles west of Kirkwall, and Standing Stones of Stenness, one mile from Brodgar. The henges are six miles from Skara Brae. Brodgar is the largest henge in the British Isles. It is surrounded by a ditch, hacked from sandstone. Stenness sits between lochs, at a point where ancient people came together. A Watch Stone, eighteen feet high, stands back from the circle, as if a territory marker. There was also a so-called Stone of Odin at Stenness, with its head-size perforation about the height of a man. Couples came to say their vows at the Stone of Odin, until it was destroyed in 1814.[9]

In contrast to life at Skara Brae, Jarlshof in Shetland experienced continuous occupation from 2500 BCE to 1600s CE. Remnants of houses from earliest residents are next to round-walled homes, like Skara Brae, occupied from 2000 BCE, through arrival of Romans in the 1st century CE. There are underground storage vaults and remnants of a 1st century CE broch, the multilevel, communal, massive stone tower. Like Skara Brae, Jarlshof is adjacent to a beach, where a retaining wall now holds back further erosion.

The broch is an impressive stone structure, standing high on the ancient landscape, much like later castles of a lord. One defensible doorway led into a three-story, double-walled tower, with a high thatched roof. Between double walls were passageways and chambers. There were sleeping areas above, and storage below, the activity area on the main floor. A broch created a building not likely to collapse in the wind, or from hostile forces.

Broches are found in each Roman era settlement. Most broches are surrounded by a wall. Within the walled courtyard there was room for animals and an outhouse.

By the 3rd century CE, Jarlshof had four wheelhouse residences, so-called for round shape and spoked beam roofs. Pebbles in the site were painted with religious symbols, including a Pictish cross, evidencing Christianity of early Scottish people. Wheelhouses were occupied until the 9th century when Vikings arrived.

In the late 9th century, a Viking family settled at Jarlshof. They built a longhouse and stone pathway, in addition to small structures. Jarlshof was a small family farm.

By the 1200s, the Viking farm was replaced by a substantial medieval farm. The farm family were likely Norse, as Shetland was then ruled from Bergen. Over centuries, the residence was enlarged, and the barn made smaller. Construction

---

9  Aubrey Burl, Rings of Stone, Ticknor & Fields, New Haven & New York, 1979, at 92-97 & 112-114.

was of drystone, that is fitted stone without mortar. High, straight walls, of rectangle buildings were of double-wall construction, in the style of the round forerunners, with a thinner soil core.

In 1469, Shetland was in control of Scottish King James III. The new lord of the land, known as laird, built a large Scottish manor house on the Jarlshof site, on top of stone structures of two to three thousand years past. Remains of the new house, with its high walls and tower, are visible today, although reduced by storms.

*St. Magnus Cathedral Kirkwall*

*Today in Shetland*

## Visiting Kirkwall and Orkney Today

Adjacent to Skara Brae is Skaill House, home of lairds of Skaill. Scottish lairds of Skaill built the two-story mansion in 1492 and filled it over the next five centuries with family heirlooms. The home is a museum. It is a timepiece, completing the story of Skara Brae.

Kirkwall is an enchanting 19th century harbor town. The town icon is St. Magnus Cathedral. Besides tourism, Kirkwall remains a fishing and shipping port for Northern Islands.

## Visiting Lerwick and Shetland Today

In the 1600s, Orkney and Shetland were under the governorship of Earl Patrick Stewart, known as *Black Patie*, for tyranny as a ruler and stripping resources from the land, historic and natural. When storms in the 1890s revealed ancient Jarlshof, locals excavated part of the site, until the government assumed management in 1925.

Jarlshof was made famous in the 1822 story, *The Pirate*, by Sir Walter Scott. Lerwick achieved celebrity in the television drama, *Shetland*. Scenes were filmed at stone cottages near the water. Neighboring homes have centuries old drystone walls.

Today Lerwick is a fishing community. Those on shore look from steep streets of their homes for family arriving from the sea. The Viking boat in the harbor, reminiscent of days of Viking arrivals, is from the annual festival of art and music. Lerwick is small, but lively.

# REPRESENTATIVE DEMOCRATIC GOVERNMENT - NORWAY TO ICELAND

## VIKING THINGS

*Thingvellir Iceland*

Iceland is home to the oldest, continual, democratic government in the world. Viking tradition of democracy inspired mass emigration from Norway to Iceland in the 9$^{th}$ century, during time of an overbearing king. Iceland was domain of Vikings transitioned to Norse farmers.

In 927, a delegate was sent from Iceland to Norway, to study law, and return to educate fellow farmers. By 930, Viking democracy, evolved from practices in Norway, was fundamental to Icelandic government. In Iceland, democracy is integral to culture.

Sophistication of Viking jurisprudence, in a representative democracy, provides a picture of Vikings in stark contrast to visions of marauders. Raiding parties and representative government were not mutually exclusive. There were rules. Transgression of rules had consequences. In a world of verbal communication, everyone knew the rules.

A millennium prior to mass communication in telephones and television, Vikings developed a means for communication through fjords. In a system rivaling the Romans, Vikings convened to learn rules, settle disputes, and become current on community affairs. So elegant was the system, that it continued into modern practice. Sessions are now held indoors, in rooms with electric lights and thermal heating. Delegates to Iceland Parliament now arrive in cars, not by ship. The Iceland Parliament sits high on a grassy hill, home to Reykjavik city government, positioned like Viking Things of old.

Vikings had an appreciation for real estate. Meeting places for legislative and judicial sessions were on rising ground, giving participants constant view of their ships. Freedoms were important. Ships were a lifeline. In Iceland, Thingvellir, a national park today, was the site of the original Icelandic Althing, the whole-island meeting, first held in 930.

Things, democratic sessions, were held in regions of Iceland, with the annual Althing held in Thingvellir.[10] This story is a vision of the critical place, where government and environment melded. Iceland has spectacular landscapes. Vikings made it special.

## Viking Democratic Tradition in Iceland

Vikings, as raiding parties of fighters in elegant ships, originated in fjords of western Norway, the Vesterland. Fiercely independent and desirous of land, competition for land amid growing populations, and a Norse king intent on subjugating Norse of Vesterland, sent able sailors west in search of new turf. In the 870s, new domain was in unoccupied Iceland. Vesterlanders joined Norse from Scotland, Orkneys, Isle of Man, and Ireland.

---

[10] Sometimes spelled Ping, with an Old Norse Character. Thingvellir is a National Park and World Heritage Site.

Ingólfr Arnarson led an armada of four hundred settlers from Norway to Iceland. They landed near present-day Reykjavik and spread across the landscape, claiming land for farms. Knowledge of their lives comes from *Icelandic Sagas*, including the *Book of Settlements*, individual stories of Norse families in the 10th and 11th centuries.[11]

From the first occupants, Iceland society was unique from others in Europe, including Scandinavia. Icelanders were farmers.[12] There were no royals. There was no demarcation by class, or hierarchy. Every farm family strove to stay alive on their land. Even the concept of slavery; captured enemies in service to a family, ended quickly in Iceland. Slavery assumed an obligation of the family to house and feed slaves. There was no excess production. Initiative and hard work kept people alive. Everyone worked on the farms.

Iceland did not develop urban centers until the 19th century. In prior centuries, farmers fed growing families, until Danes controlled Iceland and exploited fishing for export. As the population grew from immigration, there was competition for land, disputes between families over marriage and inheritance, as well as an occasional bloody encounter, all requiring resolution to keep peace. In 927, farmers nominated a fellow farmer, Ulfljótr, to sail back to fjords of western Norway to learn the law and advise Icelanders.[13]

Icelanders developed a representative democracy, surpassing the model in Norway. Norway had a constitutional monarchy, sometimes a vassal to other monarchs. Councils in Norway were local, or advisory to the monarch. In Iceland, in the absence of monarchs, or any royals, democratic councils developed into a sophisticated form of governance, without parallel in the ancient, or medieval world.

Rather than require all farmers to leave farms and meet several times each year, groups of farmers joined under a representative, who met in one of

---

[11] Norse Sagas, including *Sagas of Icelanders* and *Modruvellir*, a compellation of eleven stories of farm families, deserve their own story. Likely written by fellow farmers, they tell of loves, lives, conflicts, and peace agreements. Later *Sturlunga Saga*, of the 12th and 13th centuries, tells tales of battles.

[12] See generally, Jess Byock, Viking Age of Iceland, Penguin, London, 2001.

[13] Likely destination for Ulfljótr was Gulathing, an historic meeting place on a western fjord of Norway.

four regional meetings several times each year. In one region, there was such dissention, that it split, rendering the number of regions five by the beginning of the 11th century. A representative farmer was known as a godi, and his group of farmers were Thingmen of the godi. Godi were chiefs among fellow farmers, not royals. Being a godi was an obligation of service.

Plural of godi is godar. Godar met in in regional meetings known as a Thing. At certain times, the godar of all five regions convened in a single place. These all-Icelandic meetings were known as Althings. The first Althing, and place of Althings for centuries, was at Thingvellir. Vellir is a plain. Thingvellir, now a national park, is a large open plain, coincidentally at the edge of a great fissure in the earth, on the banks of the Axe River in central western Iceland. The site is an imposing geologic feature. Althings, regularly occurring on this landscape, were critical to formation of the nation of Iceland.

Governance in Iceland quickly developed into a three-level decision-making forum, the sort of structure touted in 21st century graduate schools of business and government. Decision-making gurus today have Vikings to thank, for devising an effective system. The outer ring of farmers, Thingmen, met with godi, one of thirty-six to forty-eight godar, to learn the law and suggest or agitate for new laws. Godar met in Things in five regions.

Regional Things convened quarterly, known as fjordungathing. A few Thingmen might attended with their godi. If godi tried to exert undue advantage over Thingmen, unhappy Thingmen could seek representation under a different godi. Although godi are referred to by historians as chiefs, Thingmen were farmers and a godi was equal among Thingmen.

From among godar, three were chosen for three-year terms to officiate at Althing. One of the three was a descendant of Ingólfr Arnarson. One of the three was supreme chief, tasked with officiating logistics of Althing. With so many people attending Thingvellir, allocation of space for meetings, tents, or turf lodges for the two-week event, and places for peddlers, brewers, and ale sellers, was necessary. The third was the law-speaker.

At Althing, high on Law Rock at Thingvellir, the law-speaker recited one-third of the laws, each of the three years of his term. If his memory failed, helpful godar assisted, no doubt fueled with ale. Votes were taken on amendments, new laws, and major decisions, such as treaties.

Althing occurred in June, when weather was best for travel. A preparatory Varthing occurred in May. At Varthing, value of an ounce in trade goods was set, known as thinglaseyrir. In a session known as skapthing, dates for Althing and procedures were established. By June, the massive Althing was set for trade deals, introduction of people to marriage prospects, and all manner of decisions made in a peaceful, orderly environment.

Icelanders had a judicial system, in tandem with the legislative process. Godi were first arbiters in dispute resolution for their Thingmen. Matters remaining contentious went to one of four regional courts. In 1005, Althing created a supreme Fifth Court.

Cases put before the Fifth Court were heard by twelve farmers appointed by godar. This may be the first instance of a jury. Although women were not godar, they were appointed to courts. The Fifth Court held two sessions annually: sóknarthing was for prosecution of criminal cases; and skuldathing was for civil actions for injury or debt. Penalty for causing harm could include payment in horses, or in the case of murder, exile. Determination of obligation for debt included failed promises of marriage and rights to marital property, or rights to property in inheritance. In Iceland, men and women were free to intermingle. Legitimacy of children was not an issue until priests arrived. Complex issues of family made for complex inheritance cases.[14]

In the 12th century, a scribe put laws into a book on pages of calfskin velum. Known as Grágás, Old Norse for Grey Goose, the book is more saga than law from Althings. Grágás does not distinguish law voted into effect at an Althing, which is legislative law, from understood social practice, which is common law.[15]

There is a section in Grágás on choice of bishop and relationship of the church in secular society, where godar are also priests. By 1118, a church building appeared on the landscape at Thingvellir. Missionary priests from Norway brought a new dimension to Iceland.

---

[14] Halldór Kiljan Laxness was awarded a Nobel Prize in Literature in 1955 for his novel, Atómstödtin (Atom Station), published in 1948, of social tension in Icelandic society. His character said she was taught to believe nothing in the newspapers, and everything in the Sagas.

[15] The book was found in the 16th century on a farm in western Iceland. It was kept in Denmark in the Old Royal Library in Copenhagen. At the time of the find, Denmark controlled Iceland.

## Separation of Church and State

In Europe, as it was in Norway, priests, particularly bishops or archbishops, held power to rival a king. In Iceland, Christianity arrived with the first settlers from Norway. Christian Icelanders looked to god in heaven, while retaining Norse gods of the sea and crops. The concept of religious and secular deity came naturally to Icelanders, while the idea of a priest or bishop as a noble fell outside the rubric of Icelandic society. The Vatican and the Archbishop of Trondheim, supreme cleric of Norway, Iceland, and eventually Greenland, had to accept a unique form of Christian practice in Iceland, to convert Icelanders.

Arrival of the church brought a need for taxes, or tithe. Godar extracted a small Thing tax from Thingmen to compensate for loss of time on the farm while attending Things. Churches held land, in competition with farmers, and required tithe to support the bishop, the local priest, the church building, and for distribution to the poor. Tithe was not distributed in equal amounts.

Norse farmers accepted Christ readily, although they balked at loss of land and payment of tithe. Church administration was not democratic. In the institution of the church versus Icelandic democracy, democracy prevailed in Iceland.

In 1173, Archbishop Eystein, sitting in his palace at Nidaros in Trondheim, refused to accept as priests any godar of Iceland, who killed a man in battle. In one edict, Eystein defrocked most godar of dual roles as Thing delegate and priest. In addition, Eystein declared priests could not advocate in a court or legislative process. The ability to defend property in court, or advocate for Thingmen, was inherent in the role of godar. In 1190, Archbishop Eirik Ivarsson refused to ordain Iceland godar as priests. The line was drawn.

At the next Althing, delegates unwound church ownership of property in Iceland. In 1195, Pal Jonsson, a priest, was elected Bishop of Iceland, at an Althing, not by a convention of priests.[16] Pal was a choice reflective of the times. He was an illegitimate child, which in Iceland carried no stigma. Pal was

---

[16] For more on Bishop Pal, see the story of Vikings Playing Chess in Cruise through History, Itinerary XII.

married and fathered several children. When he traveled to Norway, Bishop Pal was given a warm welcome by Norwegian King Sverre. Sverre became king of Norway by force, rather than by inheritance, as was custom.

By the 13th century, King Håkon unified Norway and sought expansion of his domain, to include Iceland. Norway held as vassals Orkney, Faroes, Shetlands, and Greenland, while Iceland remained independent. Håkon sent his agent Snorri Sturluson to prompt Iceland to the Norwegian fold. Snorri was part diplomat, part rabble rouser. His is also known as an author of *Norse Sagas*, including *Sturlunga Sagas* of the battles of Norway and Iceland. Snorri was not a neutral observer. He was of the Sturlung Clan, that by notoriety in saga gave the name Sturlunga Age to a time of war and loss of democracy in Iceland.[17]

At the Battle of Orlygsstadir, in 1238, in northern Iceland, Sturlung clan led one thousand warriors against seventeen hundred Icelanders. Icelanders held back invasion by the king of Norway. King Håkon tried another tactic.

At the time of battle, the godar system was deteriorating. A few men of a single family held several godar positions. They manipulated Thingmen to their advantage, as godar families dominated control of land. By controlling many Thingmen, fighting forces were formed, which was previously impossible in subsistence farming. While Snorri wrote Norse Sagas complimentary of King Håkon, the king pursued the winning Icelandic warrior, Gizur Thorvaldsson. With the king as a patron, Gizur organized Iceland, used his family crest as the island seal, and became the first jarl, that is earl of Iceland.

King Håkon died in battle attempting to attain the Hebrides and Isle of Man. Snorri died in battle in 1241. Snorri's nephew continued to write sagas. Håkon's son became King Magnus, giver of a new Law Code in 1271. Iceland remained under control of Norway when Norway became dominated by Denmark. In 1814, when Norway went from Denmark to Sweden, in the aftermath of Denmark's support for Napoleon and loss in war, Iceland remained territory of Denmark. Danish control of Iceland ended in 1944.

---

[17] See, Gunnar Karlsson, A Brief History of Iceland, Mal og menning, Reykjavik, 2016, at 16-17.

## Democracy an Integral Icelandic Tradition

Things did not end upon Gizur becoming an earl. Placement of a royal representative was important to the king of Norway. The position meant little or nothing to Icelanders. Things and Althings were ingrained in Icelandic social systems of peace keeping, justice, and regulation of property. Things were also conduits for community information, trade fairs, and places of social interaction. If Things were not important to kings of Norway, they held meaning for Icelanders.

There are no sagas recording a list of Law-Speakers after 1271, when King Magnus of Norway gave a constitution of sorts to Iceland. Of record is the 1845 decree of King Christian VIII of Denmark, which allowed Things to advise the Danish governor of Iceland. In 1873, an Althing asked the Danish king for a new constitution. A statue in front of the historic government house in Reykjavik, also residence of Danish royal representatives, shows King Christian IX giving Iceland a constitution, which allowed Things as advisory to the Danish Minister for Iceland. Icelanders did not need political decrees of foreign nations to know their identity. Personal freedom and local decision-making emanated from established practice.

Norway was part of the Kalmar Union, a triumvirate of Norway, Sweden, and Denmark, in which Denmark was supreme. From the 1480s Iceland was Denmark's domain. Denmark ruled Iceland as a source of fish, crops, and wool exploited for the benefit of Denmark. Iceland was divided into trade districts, in which only Danes could participate in trade.

Foreign ships brought disease to Iceland. In 1707 there was a small-pox epidemic and in other years plague. In 1751 to 1758, there were crop failures and famine, when exports to Denmark of fish and grain continued. In 1783 there was a volcanic eruption, followed the next year by earthquakes, leaving a haze over the sky, which caused more famine.

By the beginning of the 19th century the Iceland population stood at forty thousand. Hundreds of farms perished in volcanic activity and earthquakes. Through political overlords, environmental disaster, and introduction of disease, Icelanders persevered. They maintained farms, Norse language, and their heritage of a democratic society.

In 1918, Denmark agreed to home rule for Iceland. By 1920, a national court system was in force. Althings moved indoors to the Parliament Building in Reykjavik. The Parliament Building has an Art Deco style typical of the time in Europe. Women heads of households were voting members of Things since 1882. By 1911, women had equal rights to education. In a 1920 census, the urban population exceeded rural population. Reykjavik had a population of twenty thousand.

June 17, 1944 is National Day in Iceland. On that date, Denmark gave Iceland independence. A celebration of independence was held at Thingvellir.

## Visiting Reykjavik Today

Iceland needed no political capital of the realm when all legislative and judicial business was transacted in Things and at Althing in Thingvellir. In a land of farmers, there were no urban centers. Urban centers developed at the direction of Danish kings for use as ports.

As proof of ongoing importance of Things to Icelanders, in 1751, Skuli Magnusson and a dozen like-minded farmers requested approval at a Thing for the establishment of a commercial enterprise. *Innrettinger*, the New Enterprises, was a factory near the harbor in Reykjavik, to weave wool for export. This first commercial homestead, near where the first settlers landed eight hundred years earlier, became the beginning of Reykjavik as the economic capital of Iceland.

In 1786, Denmark ended its monopoly of trade. Icelanders flourished in business. Skuli Magnusson is regarded as the father of Reykjavik. Icelanders consider 1786 the year of city founding. By 1800, there were five shops in Reykjavik. The population grew to more than three hundred residents. Today one-third of Iceland's population lives in Reykjavik.

Today, the inner harbor of Reykjavik is serene. A small fort is overshadowed by the Harpa, a stunning concert hall. A seawall monument is dedicated to slipping off to sea to end lives, spent in rough and beautiful, unspoiled Icelandic landscape. Above the harbor a forest of cranes marks a boom in construction. Mainstreet is still a row of low profile, wood buildings from the harbor to the lake. Around the lake are lovely estate homes.

Parliament is at the top of a hill, where Old Government House is at the bottom. Buildings are heated by natural steam. To see steam at the source, see waterfalls, geysers, and the Blue Lagoon thermal spa. Travel to Thingvellir National Park, where the landscape is ready to host an Althing. A lucky few will view Northern Lights.

## Eric and Leif

Thus far this story of Iceland has not included exploits of Eric the Red and his son Leif Ericson. Names familiar to those in the United States as synonymous with Iceland are out of touch with Icelanders, who consider the men rogue sidelights to history. Eric was born near Stavanger, Norway in 950. When he was ten, Eric's father, Thorvald Asvaldsson, committed murder for which he was exiled to Iceland. Iceland as a repository for criminals from Norway has never found much appreciation in Iceland.

By the time Eric's family arrived in Iceland, all the good farmland was occupied by Norse families. Eric married into a respectable family and inherited a fine farm. Eric also inherited his father's temper. After causing the death of two men, Eric was sentenced at a Thing to three years exile in Greenland from 982.

Contrary to typical American history accounts of Eric, he did not discover Greenland. The Icelandic Sagas give credit to Gunnbjörn Ulfson for discovery. Eric returned to Iceland extolling virtues of land available in Greenland, a name he assigned to make it appealing. As head of a large, now respectable family, Eric led a convoy to settle Greenland. Emigrating with Eric was his twelve-year-old son Leif. As an adult, Leif made haphazard sailings from Norway to Greenland, bypassing Iceland. He sailed with able Viking mariners foraging timber in North America, for which he is given credit for the discovery five hundred years prior to Columbus.

In 1930, the United States commissioned a statue of Leif Ericson, by sculptor Alexander Stirling Calder, to commemorate a millennium of democratic government in Iceland, from 930. Choice of subject was curious to Icelanders. They placed the American gift at the entrance to the US military compound. When the land reverted to Reykjavik, the city moved the statue to a traffic circle and used the former military area for a cathedral.

Travel opens the mind and senses. For those traveling to Iceland, lasting impressions will include amazing landscapes, dramatic waterfalls, and broad vistas. Thingvellir National Park, at the cusp of a fissure in the earth, hosted enduring democracy. Eric who? Leif who? It really does not matter. Take photos to treasure with Ingólfr Arnarson.

*Ingólfr Arnarson- Icelandic Image of Icelander*

*Leif Erickson – American Image of Icelander*

*Cuchulainn tied to a post facing enemies- In Dublin Post Office*

# DOMESTIC RELATIONS – DUBLIN

## *Táin bó Cuailnge* – The Cattle Raid of Cooley

In the 6th century monks copied scripture into beautifully illustrated manuscripts, such as the Book of Kells.[18] They also recorded epic poetry, containing creation stories, tales of heroes, and early kings of Ireland. A famous Irish epic poem is the *Táin bó Cuailnge*, also known as the Cattle Raid of Cooley. It is to the Táin that nationalist writers and politicians turned in the 18th through 20th centuries for a sense of Irishness.

A cattle raid in an obscure area seems unlikely material for a national poem. This was a selective raid, for a special bull, property of the leading lady of ancient Ireland, the queen of Connaught, Maeve.[19] She was responsible for the death of her sister, when the sister was pregnant. The child survived to avenge his mother's death by shooting Maeve with a piece of cheese, shot from his slingshot, while the queen was bathing. Translation from Old Irish to English was "cheese." No doubt something was lost in translation.

The bull of this story was taken by Maeve's ex-husband, the king of Ulster, Concobar.[20] Before the bull is retrieved and taken back to Connaught, the poem winds through side stories, humorous tales of real people, and comes to a crescendo moment of the Irish tragic hero. The story begins as a tragic love story, moves through a side story of magic and a curse, then returns to the central issue between Maeve and Concobar: ownership of the bull upon separation of their marital assets.

---

[18] The original is on display in Trinity College Library in Dublin.
[19] Also spelled Madb. Connaught is western Ireland. Maeve is the goddess of war and fertility.
[20] Ulster is Northern Ireland. Concobar in Old Irish became Connor, or O'Connor.

As the story goes: King Concobar was to marry Deidre. Deidre, however, fell in love with Naisi. The lovers left Ireland in the company of Naisi's two brothers and were married. A loyal servant to king Concobar, the able warrior, Fergus, convinced the lovers that Concobar had calmed, making it safe to return to Ireland. Relying upon the guarantee of Fergus, the lovers returned.

Concobar still had strong feelings for Deidre. Upon seeing his love, Concobar pulled Deidre into his castle and killed the three brothers. Deidre killed herself. Deidre recurs as a theme in Irish poetry and song as Deidre of the Sorrows. Fergus either killed himself in shame or headed west joining ranks with Maeve. He is no longer critical to the plot.

Meanwhile, a new group of characters enter the poem as sub-story. In the story of the Supernatural Bride, a bride of wondrous strength required her husband to keep their lives private to remain happy in their village. Unable to control himself, the husband bragged to village men that his wife could run faster than Concobar's horses. The men challenged the husband to prove his boast or be killed. Ever supportive of her husband, the bride, though pregnant, displayed her speed in a race with the king's horses. Having proven the boast and saved her husband's life, the bride is fatally weakened. As she dies, she curses men of Concobar's army with debilitation. The curse took immediate effect.

Maeve decided time was ripe to invade Ulster and retrieve her bull, while the king's warriors were debilitated by the curse. The queen's army was led by Ferdinand, a suiter of Maeve's daughter, Finnabair. King Concobar had no defenses to meet the invading army, except for one aristocrat, who was unaffected by the curse. The splendid warrior was the semi-divine, Achilles-like, super-warrior, Cuchulainn.

Cuchulainn received many blows, which did not vanquish him. He alone defended Concobar's interests in the bull. To remain standing to fight, while he was weak from the effort, Cuchulainn lashed himself to a pillar. His death came when a crow landed on his shoulder to drink his blood. When Cuchulainn was observed too weak to brush off the crow, the king's army advanced. Statues depict Cuchulainn at a pillar, with crows.

Although an aristocrat in service to the king, in 18th through 20th century revivals of the tales, Cuchulainn is a man of the people. In retelling of the medieval Book of Leinster, Cuchulainn accepts death, in a moment of chivalry, so long as his deeds are not forgotten. His wish is granted.

*Salmon of Knowledge in Belfast*

In the 6th through 12th centuries, Christian monks removed fairies from Irish folk tales, as they copied texts on velum in monasteries. In the 19th century, poet William Butler Yeats and playwright Lady Isabella Augusta Gregory put fairies back into action.[21] Yeats, the national poet of Ireland, claimed that to know Ireland, it was necessary to read its poems as originally told.

In Yeats' works, Cuchulainn is an icon of the common man of Ireland, who vanquished oppressors. In 1890, Yeats returned from England to his native Dublin, where his work epitomized Irish Nationalism in poetry. He stood back from violence escalating around him, preferring text and theatrical productions promoting Irish culture. His acceptance speech for the Nobel Prize in Literature in 1923, highlighted Irish history.

Yeats, Lady Gregory, and playwright Edmund John Millington Synge founded the Abbey Theatre in Dublin.[22] The Abbey was such a popular venue for Irish

---

[21] Yeats 1865 to 1939, Dublin and Gregory 1852 to 1932, Galway.
[22] Edmund John Millington Synge 1871 to 1909 in Dublin.

nationalist themes in plays, it was blamed in part for igniting uprisings in 1916, that culminated in creation of the National Republic of Ireland. Synge's production of The Playboy of the Western World in 1907, was cut short by a riot of theatergoers.

Irish storytelling continued from ancient myths into the Christian era, joining morality tales and romance stories. Stories of the 3$^{rd}$ century family of Finn MacCuhal, or MacCool, are known as Finnian Stories. Finn is not an aristocrat or a warrior/hero. He is a popular folk hero, who is crafty and resourceful, vindictive, but generous. Finn's stories are humorous and romantic. When an enemy of Finn threw water on him from a magic well, he simply swallowed the water and became endowed of special powers. He ate the Salmon of Knowledge, which made him wise. Thus began the idea that eating fish makes you smart.

Irish filí, the storytellers, arrived with fairies in Ireland, long before lawyers. Retrieving marital property in a dissolution required heroism of Cuchulainn. Today, the Salmon of Knowledge served with a pint of Guinness goes a long way towards resolving disputes.

# INTELLECTUAL PROPERTY/ COPYRIGHT –
## IRELAND/SCOTLAND
### St. Columba and the Book of Kells

*St. Columba's Iona with St. Martin's High Cross in foreground*

Irish filí provided entertainment in early Ireland. They were so insinuated in society they could command patronage of a lord. Overcome with their own importance, filí imposed until they wore out their welcome. Faced with banishment, filí appealed to a leader of the poet's guild, Colum-cille, known to Scots as St. Columba, defender of the word.

Columba was a poet-monk, dedicated to copying books, in the tradition of 6th century monks. He lived in Ireland until he came to blows with a lord. Columba was copying a book owned by the lord. When finished, Columba believed the copy was his, but the lord disagreed. The lord asserted the copy was part of the original, inseparable, and thus property of the lord. The argument was a contest of intellectual property and copyright.

Columba became the warrior-monk, ready to battle for the book. He won the battle, keeping his life, but lost the war. He was banished, traveled to Iona, in Scotland, and became a patron saint of the Scots.

Columba knew the worth of filí. He is regarded as saying that if there were no poets to praise the king, the king would merely be remembered as "a skull and letters on a stone."[23] Columba also cautioned poets with outsized images of their worth, that they had a responsibility to well tell the tale. He likely said,

> If the poet's verse be fable,
> Then is all your knowledge fable.
> All your rights and state and power,
> And this drifting world is fable.[24]

The saint recognized a good story contains enough truth to be credible. The Irish always knew stories were not literally true. For them, politicians were no different than storytellers. In Ireland, poets and politicians are all filí.

## Mystique of Iona

Iona is a magical place. Pilgrims, monks, hermits, kings, conquerors, mystics, and vacation travelers have been drawn to this place since Columba founded his out-post of self-exile from Ireland in 565 CE. There are so many legends associated with this spot, that each stone on this island in the Irish Sea glows in sacred light, of an ethereal force. There is rarely sunshine Iona. Clouds hang low in deference to sanctity of the place.

---

[23] A Treasury of Irish Folklore, ed. Padraic Colum, Wings Books, New York, 1967, at 129.
[24] Id at 30.

Separating myth or fact from interwoven folk tales, or 18th century hype, is difficult. Columba lived in sparse accommodations. In the 9th century, relics of value were removed or hidden from Viking raiders. Structures date from the 12th to 16th century. Though existing buildings have historic caché, they date after Columba's exit.

Still, Iona was Columba's chosen place. The Book of Kells began in Iona. For a millennium, kings desired eternal glory by burial in the Iona cemetery. When so many real and secular people of power are drawn to a single place, the aura has veracity.

Reaching Iona today requires commitment to travel to a remote island, with few resources. Most days are cold and wet. Few ferries arrive and they stay just a few minutes at the little dock. Townsfolk know it is not a delightful destination. A warming room near the pier is always open for travelers waiting to depart.

Ever present clouds over the abbey add to its mystique. Stark, stone-grey buildings evoke a proper mood, that a sunny day makes inauthentic. Absent cold, wet, and windy weather, Iona would not be a monk's self-effacing habitat.

When visiting Iona, it is best to wear old shoes, a tightly held hat, and a raincoat. It is also good to go armed with background on Columba and his monastery. Cult-like enthusiasm is not necessary. Mild curiosity is sufficient. Feel the sensation of walking in a place where living beings are not alone.

## St. Columba – Real and Mythical

According to legend, Columba came face-to-face with the Loch Ness Monster and the monster blinked first. In death, Columba's miracles accumulated, until sainthood was assured. St. Columba had a good press agent.

It is fact that St. Columba made Iona his base, from which he planned to Christianize pagans of Scotland. In matters of faith, truth is not a qualifier for adulation. Destiny of the man was cast when he went to war over a book.

On the River Boyne in Ireland, not far from ancient burial mounds made before Celts came to Ireland, and predating Stonehenge, some Irish souls melded into the Christian era in Clonard Abbey. In this place, in the 6th century, twelve young men gathered under the tutelage of Finnian of Clonard. Finnian was a priest trained under Martin of Tours in Gaul, in the pious, reverent manner of a self-effacing teacher.

Finnian returned to his native Ireland, where he founded a teaching monastery, which quickly attracted young monks. Finnian is regarded as St. Finnian, teacher of the Twelve Apostles of Ireland. His students distinguished themselves as founders of monasteries, throughout Ireland and Scotland.[25] One of the Irish Apostles was St. Columba.[26]

In his birthplace in Ireland, in 521, he was known as Colum cille, meaning church dove in Gaelic. His original name was Crimthann, the fox. Whether Columba was a fox or dove depends on who writes his history. In the 6th century a man was a farmer, warrior, or monk. Columba was a warrior-monk. Boisterous and outspoken, he could also be pious and reverent. Monasteries fostered reverence and he was schooled in a monastery.

Monks spent time in monasteries painstakingly copying portions of the Bible into psalters, portions of gospels. In Clonard Abbey, under Finnian, Columba copied a psalter that Finnian brought to Ireland. Columba was pleased with his effort, until Finnian assumed ownership of the work. Finnian was head of the abbey, owner of the original, and thus claimed ownership of the copy. Columba's disappointment reached a non-monastic level of outrage.

In what may be the first copyright battle, Columba and Finnian laid their disagreement before the king of Tara, high king of Ireland. King Diarmait was a pagan, inaugurated on Tara hill, who became a Christian. That two Christian clerics brought their grievance to him was an affirmation that as a Christian, he was still law of the land.

---

[25] The difference between monastery and abbey is in function. Monasteries are places of refuge and study by a group of monks. Monasteries are self-sufficient and include a chapel. Some monasteries grow into abbeys, in which a priest designee is abbot. Abbeys may include a monastery and public community church and school.

[26] One of the Twelve Apostles was St. Brendan the Navigator, who went on a journey, searching for the Island of Paradise. St. Brendan's Island is a mythical place off North Africa. He met St. Columba and told him of sightings of a sea monster, possibly from Lock Ness. Patron saints of Ireland are St. Patrick, St. Columba, and St. Brigid of Kildare.

King Diarmait pondered the question of ownership of a work, meticulously copied from, to be fair, a copy of a copy of a psalter brought from France. The king took jurisdiction over the case placed before him. He ruled that every cow owns her calf. In a land of farmers, natural law was primary. Finnian was determined owner of the book.

The dispute took place in 560, when political discord brewed between King Diarmait and clan Uí Néill. Clan Uí Néill were contenders for rulers of Tara, as descendants of King Néill, king of Tara in the prior century. Columba was of clan Uí Néill. No doubt, he cried judicial bias. In the 6th century, forum for appeal of a king's decision was the battlefield.

The Battle of Cúl Dreimhne, in northwest Ireland, Connaught County, is known as the Battle of the Book. At stake to warriors, few of whom were literate, was insult to their clan, that became political. Columba's dispute with his mentor, and appeal to his clan, touched an explosive cord in religious and secular communities.

During the battle[27], a cousin of Columba, named Curman, killed a relative of King Diarmait. Curman sought refuge with Columba, in the monastery at Kells, Ireland. Church as refuge was a new concept in 560. Diarmait's clan did not acknowledge such a safe zone. Curman was ripped from Columba's protective arms and killed. Three thousand combatants lost their lives in the Battle of the Book.

Whether Columba instigated the battle or contributed a fuse to existing hostility between clans seeking control of Tara, he took responsibility for the deaths. Columba knew he must leave Ireland. Under no circumstances could he return to the Abbey of Finnian. Columba sailed north into the Hebrides, until he could no longer see Ireland. He landed on Iona, a tiny island off the Isle of Mull, where he founded a monastery. Columba's penance was to Christianize Picts in Scotland, saving as many souls for Christ as died in the Battle of the Book.

As a postscript to the Battle of the Book, the psalter copied by Columba, known as Cathach of St. Columba, was preserved by O'Donnell clan, rivals of

---

[27] Curman either caused the death during battle, or in a sporting event, a hurling match, or in team riots after the match. Hurlers of the time used large, disc-shaped rocks.

O'Neill clan. The Cathach was in the monastery at Kells in the 11th century when it was given a gilded cover. The Abbot of Kells was of O'Donnell clan, which may explain custody. Rediscovered and authenticated in 1830, the book is revered today as the oldest surviving manuscript. It is in the collection of the Royal Irish Academy in Dublin.

## St. Columba - the Lovely Bones

Columba was not the only Irish monk converting pagans in Ireland and Scotland. He was also not the first monk on Iona. Upon Columba's arrival on Iona in 565, he and the monastery were linked in the pantheon of Irish Christian history. A large abbey was built on the remote island of a small population, because it was the monastery of St. Columba.

Most of what is known, or believed, of St. Columba in Scotland is due to the book, *The Life of Columba*, written by the monk Adomnán, in 697, a century after death of the saint. Adomnán wrote that Columba came to Iona with twelve companions, among them Oran.[28] Iona Abbey kept Columba out of sight of Ireland. Land for a monastery was given to Columba by a clansman, an Irish king of Día Riata, as Scotland was then known.

Adomnán was the ninth Abbot of Iona. For his book he drew upon records kept by prior abbots and monks. Cumulative information became a *Vita Columbae*, that is, a resumé of Columba supporting his veneration as a saint. Whether incidents described are faith or facts, they are the information upon which historians and the church rely.

In his travels across the Loch at Ness, Columba came across a group of people distressed by a dying young man on the shore of the Loch, who had an encounter with a sea monster. As Columba looked over the water, the sea monster surfaced to face the future saint. Columba made the sign of the cross and told the creature to be gone. The creature let out a tremendous howl and disappeared below the water, never to be seen again.

Next, Columba traveled to the castle of a Pictish king. Passing his hand over the locks (not lochs) to the castle gate, the locks opened. Astounded by such power in a man of God, the king converted to Christianity. Most Picts were not so easily converted.

---

[28] Oran is also known as Odran.

Columba reportedly predicted victories in battles and deaths. Most famously, he predicted his own death, in Iona, in 597. Monks of Iona saw light of the heavens shine on Columba as he said his final prayers. Never has veneration of Columba been questioned.[29]

Bones of Saint Columba were placed in a silver reliquary, a little carrying box. The lovely bones of the saint exerted power in death as the saint displayed during life. The reliquary of St. Columba traveled through Europe in 753.[30] It was taken by Robert the Bruce into the Battle of Bannokburn in 1314, where outnumbered Scottish forces triumphed over the English. During religious wars of the 16th century Reformation, relics of the saint were lost.

Columba was not a missionary. It is unlikely he brought three thousand souls to Christianity in atonement for deaths at the Battle of Cúl Dreimhne. There is no doubt Columba was a man of books. At Iona monastery manuscripts were created. In travels of Columba to Kells, and in his trip to Ireland and the monastery at Durrow, great manuscripts were copied.[31]

The Book of Durrow was compiled fifty years after Columba's death. Its artwork began in the monastery in Iona, or Lindisfarne. In lore of the Book of Kells, it was begun in Iona Monastery.[32] It is difficult to determine which artists trained in one monastery and collaborated on a book in another monastery.

There is no doubt that Columba inspired compilation of illuminated manuscripts.[33] His first copied psalter precipitated events which began his travels, culminating in his veneration. Other monks could dream of following his path.

---

[29] In the 6th century veneration was by general acclamation. Catholic.org and Catholic Encyclopedia, - St. Columba.
[30] See, Peter Yeoman and Nicki Scott, Iona, Historic Scotland Pub., 2016.
[31] Book of Durrow, 650 and Book of Kells 9th century. Both are on display in the University of Dublin library.
[32] Geoff Holder, The Guide to Mysterious Iona and Staffa, The History Press, UK, 2007, 2011, at 60.
[33] Illuminated manuscripts, such as Kells and Durrow, have elaborate artwork inked into velum pages.

*St. Oran's Chapel at Iona*

# NON-BELLIGERENTS IN WAR – IONA

## Bishop Adomnán's Law of Innocents

On June 9, 597, Columba died at Iona. Shortly after publication of Adomnán's book *The Life of St. Columba*, in 697, a shrine to Saint Columba was built, not far from his grave, at the site of St. Oran's Chapel today. Prominence of Iona Abbey soared as a popular pilgrimage site. Adomnán's stature grew with the Abbey.

Columba's long list of saintly acts grew longer after his death, aided by Adomnán. Columba prophesied victories in battle and deaths, confirmed in the biography. Heavenly apparitions appeared, miracles happened, and good crops rose blessed by Columba.

Abbot Adomnán was a scholar, prior to elevation at Iona. Being abbot required overcoming competition. He is a sidenote to history without Iona association. Iona's connection to St. Columba gave it fame aided by and to the benefit of Adomnán.

Another notable effort of Abbot Adomnán was *Law of the Innocents*, written in 697. In the book, Adomnán made a case for protection of non-combatant women, children, and clergy during times of war. His book was the law of the land in Ireland and Scotland, until supplanted by British law.[34] Adomnán negotiated return of hostages after battles.

---

[34] Consider Adomnán's Law of the Innocents a forerunner of Abraham Lincoln's Civil War era Lieber Code.

Pilgrims come to Iona seeking strength from proximity to Columba. They look for his stone writing table, in his dwelling on the hill in the graveyard. They look in vain for items existing only in legend. Although, Columba founded Iona monastery and much writing occurred there, his remains rested many years in the church crypt until veneration. Columba's pillow refers to a gravestone marker, part of posthumous Columba lore. Dwelling hill is the remnant of a Roman wall, indicating strategic importance of Iona prior to arrival of monks.

In 634, Saxon King Oswald invited monks from Iona to begin a community at Lindisfarne, an island off the northeast coast of England, known as Holy Island. The monastery holds infamous distinction as victim of the first Viking raid in England in 793. From success in collecting valuable loot from unprotected monks, Vikings began two centuries of raids.

Iona was a repeated Viking target. Vikings came in 795, 802, and 805. In 805, several monks met martyrdom by refusing to divulge location of Columba's relics. Vikings valued the silver carrying container, the reliquary, more than bones of the saint. By 900, Vikings were resident farmers in Dublin. Several were Christian. A raid during Christmas mass in 986, was an errant group of Danes. By the 11th century, the Viking era was history and lore.

A sidenote to Viking raids, and an indication of the sanctity with which Iona was regarded, a Viking is interred on the Iona beach, near the graveyard. Identity of the deceased is not known. Though precious items in the chapel were looted, Vikings appreciated sanctity of the graveyard. Iona imbues all comers with feelings of reverence.

## The Resting Place of Kings, in Myth and Fact

St. Oran's Chapel was built over the gravesite of St. Columba in the 11th century. St. Oran was a monk who traveled from Kells to Iona with Columba. Chapels were dedicated in the name of a saint. Oran agreed to martyr himself by being buried alive on the site, as the first of Columba's monks to die in Iona. The martyrdom of Oran is not verified by archaeology of the site. The legend was sufficient to venerate Oran and dedicate a chapel.

*Iona Graveyard of Vikings and Scottish Kings*

The present chapel dates to 1164, the bequest of Roland Somerled, self-proclaimed King of the Isles. For two centuries, the chapel was the resting place of Somerled kings. The snug stone building replaced older chapels. Iona needed repair after Viking raids. Several kings of Scotland contributed to repair and expand Iona Abbey. Scottish kings, monks, and abbots were buried in the church graveyard, dating to the Columba era.

There are more legends than confirmed burials of Scottish kings in Iona. That Scotland was so often in turmoil, and stories are numerous, give credibility to royal burials. Kenneth, king of Picts, first king of Dál Riada, kingdom of Scotland, was buried in Iona. Stories tell that kings Malcolm, Duncan, Macbeth, and Donald were interred there.[35]

In 1200, Benedictine monks were invited to Iona, despite historic animosity between Benedictines and Columbian monks. Lord Somerled of the time, the abbey patron, wanted a vibrant, working order at Iona. Augustinian nuns were also invited to Iona.

---

[35] The most recent burial was in 1994, of John Smith a member of the British Parliament, who was fond of Iona.

## Visiting Iona Today

By 1499, Bishop of the Isles was of the Campbell clan. Five hundred years later, the 8th Duke of Argyll, George Campbell, transferred ownership of Iona Abbey to an abbey trust. In 2000, Historic Scotland purchased the property from the trust, to continue preservation, restoration, and management as a visitor site. Although the abbey had extensive restoration in the 20th century, enough of the 12th and 14th century construction exists to make a visit enchanting.

All that remains of the convent is a few walls near the ferry landing. One wall displays convent humor, where *Sheela-na-gig*, the woman with raised skirts, smirks at passersby. The sign was intended to ward off evil. Nuns supported themselves providing services to pilgrims. After the Protestant Reformation closed Catholic institutions, noble women still preferred burial in Iona Abbey graveyard.

Between the convent and ticket booth to the abbey is Maclean's Cross. The carving was commissioned in 1400, as a signpost for pilgrims. It is carved of a single stone, possibly from a ring of standing stones. People lived on Iona before Celts and Druids. Celtic ring-headed high cross, St. John Cross, carved between 600 and 800, is the oldest ring cross known. St. Martin's High Cross, a ring cross, cast its shadow over St. Columba's shrine for twelve centuries.

Visitors walking steppingstones from the church to the graveyard, are treading the Way of Death. Funeral processions walked along these stones. Macbeth's body came this way.

There is more to explore on Iona beyond the Abbey. Walk the island viewing wildlife. Sunny days are rare. Dark and windy weather suits spirits of Iona. Iona is the final resting place of wandering monks and warring Scottish kings. Absorb it all before the chill forces a visit to the café and gift shop by the ferry landing. Remember, ferries are few and boarding time is brief.

# CIVIL CODE (POLITICAL LICENSE) – SCOTLAND

## Code of Macbeth vs Shakespeare's Macbeth

*Glamis Castle of Macbeth Fame*

Macbeth was a real king of Scotland. He lived, loved, and fought foes in the 11th century. His fame arises, not from victory in battle, able leadership of his people, or a legacy in formation of Scotland. The king is best known for the 17th century portrayal in a play written by William Shakespeare. In six centuries from the life of a benevolent Celtic king, who traveled to Rome to meet with the pope, to his story retold on stage in London, he went from hero to villain. It is the Shakespearean view of the king that is preserved in history. The real Macbeth needed a better press agent.

Macbeth of Shakespeare is political prose. The Bard created masterful works of art to delight audiences. His productions required a sponsor, regardless of contemporary popularity of his plays. Then, as now, theatrical productions were expensive. Shakespeare knew his patrons well. Macbeth was written to its sponsor, the newly crowned king of England, the Scottish king. Any corruption of factual history was accepted. The Globe was a theater, not a classroom. Macbeth performances sold well.

Bloody battles defined the times in which kings, such as Macbeth, maintained power. Conquer or be conquered was the rule of the day. The real Macbeth was a victor in battle in response to an aggressor. The aggressive loser was ancestor to the new king of England.

When Queen Elizabeth I died in 1603, her successor, James I, attained power in the style of the times, by inheritance. Although less bloody, intrigue surrounded succession to the throne. Being Scottish, James needed a public relations boost. The concept of a united Great Britain was in its infancy. Validating the right of a Scot to the crown of England was a challenge Shakespeare embraced.

Portraying James as a legitimate king required clarifying his ancestors' Scottish royal pedigree. The real Macbeth became literary carnage. Bloody battles in the woods offered opportunity for great drama. Inclusion of a few real events rendered fiction believable.

Besides being a brilliant playwright, Shakespeare was a fabulous travel writer. He often set plays in real places, well known to his audiences. The setting for Macbeth is Glamis Castle in Scotland, north of Edinburgh. Glamis has a pedigree, apart from Macbeth. At Glamis, fact and fiction blend, making the castle a Scotland visitor favorite.

## The Real Macbeth in Scottish History

Macbeth's story is iconic of early kings of Scotland. Six hundred years before Shakespeare, when Scotland was known as land of Alba, bands of Gaelic people roamed the forests, fished the lochs, and grew wheat. Romans called the people Picts, for their painted faces, although Scots prefer the reference tied to tartan tunics, beginning a Scottish tradition.

Small kingdoms developed in Alba, led by clan chiefs. Clan chiefs were father figures, who led people in battles to secure land, rather than royals by birth. Homeland was a fluid concept. Allegiance to chiefs was earned by able leadership, defined as strong and fair.

Around 500 CE, Celt brothers Fergus, Angus, and Lorne MacErc moved into Alba from Ireland and established the Scottish capital of Dál Riada (Argyll). New Scots and ancient Picts quarreled between them and among themselves. Spilling blood was the preferred method of dispute resolution. Any assumption of Scots conquering Picts should be avoided. Rather, the groups intermarried to the point of blended heritage.

In the 9th century, clan chiefs choose a high king to unite clans against common foes, notably Vikings. In 843, Kenneth MacAlpin, king of Dál Riada, land of Scots, was chosen high king. He was also high king of Picts when he married into the Pict royal family. Vikings devastated Pict coastal settlements. Kenneth gained fame by ousting Vikings.

A descendant of Kenneth, Malcolm Forranch, known as Malcolm the Destroyer, became King Malcolm II. He made his mark by ousting Angles and Saxons. Malcolm famously held off Viking King Canute of England in the Battle of Carham in 1018. By 1034, Malcolm extended Scotland to its present borders. Turf was divided into seven provinces, headed by mormaers, or mayors. Mormaer of Ross and Moray, a great territory, was Macbeth.

As a young man, Macbeth MacFindley was an aide to Malcolm during the Battle of Carham. In Gaelic, Macbeth is MacBeatha, meaning son of life. His mother adored him. Macbeth married into Scottish royalty when he married Gruoch, whose father Kenneth III and brother were killed by Malcolm.[36]

Macbeth was an honorable man by 11th century Scotland standards. He became mormaer by burning to death his cousin, the assassin of his father, along with fifty of his cousin's men. Macbeth then married Gruoch, his deceased cousin's widow.

---

[36] Kenneth III died in 994, not in battle, rather by biting into a poison apple, a gift brought to him by the beautiful mother of his predecessor, on behalf of Malcolm, his successor. Walt Disney did not invent the poison apple story.

As a popular descendant of the founding MacErc brothers, and as a powerful mormaer, Macbeth was next in line for king of Scotland. Instead, Malcolm anointed his nephew, Duncan. Duncan was as treacherous as Malcolm, with less skill.[37]

Duncan made enemies when he invaded England, before attacking neighbors in Scotland. Then he attacked his cousin Thorfinn of Orkney. In each skirmish, Duncan lost the battle and diminished his reputation as a leader. In 1040, Duncan attacked Macbeth.

On the battlefield, Duncan aged twenty-seven and Macbeth aged forty fought with swords. Macbeth was caught between Duncan and the scorched-earth Celtic king of Dublin. Duncan and Macbeth wounded each other. When fighting paused, the Dublin king went home and Duncan, a hemophiliac, bled to death. Macbeth was elected king.

Macbeth was anointed king on the Stone of Destiny at Scone. Scotland enjoyed relative peace. Macbeth exiled Duncan's two sons by 1042, fended off attacks by Duncan's father in 1046, and kept Viking king Thorfinn within Orkney. In 1054, another of Duncan's sons, Malcolm Canmore, known as Big Head, fostered discontent in Macbeth's domain.

Macbeth was a good king, an efficient administrator, and a benevolent Christian. He was the first Scottish king credited with establishing a rule of civil law to settle disputes, in place of bloody brawls. Law of Macbeth, resolution of disputes by arguments placed before a just king, was a legacy. Macbeth met the pope in Rome where he displayed civilized Scottish society. He was generous in alms distributed to the poor.

Gruoch was a gracious hostess and a supportive partner to Macbeth. The couple had no children. Macbeth adopted his stepson, Lulach, and instituted tanistry, royal succession through the mother. Lulach was not concerned that Macbeth killed his natural father. They were a happy and functional, 11$^{th}$ century family, until Canmore's persistent assaults.

---

[37]  For bloody details see: Magnus Magnusson, The Story of a Nation, Grove Press, New York, 2000; Nigel Tranter, The Story of Scotland, Nelson Wilson Publishing, Glasgow, 1987, 2012; Fitzroy MacLean, Scotland: A Concise History, Thames Hudson, New York, 1993; and Fiona Watson, Macbeth: A True Story, Quercus, London, 2010.

In the first recorded use of camouflage in warfare, Birnam Wood came to Dunsinane in 1054.[38] Canmore's troops used cut leafy branches to hide their advance on Macbeth's army. In the battle, Macbeth was not vanquished. He eluded Canmore for three years.

Finally, Macbeth was ensnared. Malcolm watched MacDuff, Earl of Fife, slay the king. Six months later, Malcolm killed Lulach, the final hurdle to becoming Malcolm III.

Macbeth was interred in Iona. Scotland hobbled through an era of progeny of Malcolm III and his six sons, with Saxon names, by his second wife, Margaret.[39] The sixth son, David, rebuilt Scotland, and reinstituted Laws of Macbeth.

## Shakespeare's Macbeth

In Shakespeare's Macbeth, Duncan is a good king. Macbeth is a knight in service to his king who becomes a traitor. Upon return from victorious encounters with Vikings, Macbeth and fellow knight Banquo encounter three witches. The first witch identifies Macbeth as lord of Glamis castle, the second identifies Macbeth as lord of an additional castle, which he does not then possess, and the third predicts that he will soon be king.

When Macbeth learns of a bequest to him of property of a fallen knight, he realizes two of the three pronouncements are true. He advises his ambitious wife of the prophesy of witches and the king's upcoming visit to their castle. Although Macbeth is reluctant to employ treachery, his wife plays upon his darker side. He kills the king. Out, Out, Damn Spot, they cry, when stained by the king's blood. Duncan's sons flee the country.

During the encounter with witches, Banquo was told he would never be king, although he would "beget" kings, that is, have royal progeny. To secure his crown, Macbeth engages assassins to kill Banquo and his son. Banquo is killed.

---

[38] The site of the battle has been further identified as Lumphanan, in Aberdeenshire.
[39] Sons of Malcolm III and Margaret of Hungary were Edward, Ethelred, Edmund, Edgar, Alexander, and David. Margaret brought a piece of the True Cross to Scotland and is revered as a saint in an Edinburgh Castle chapel.

His son escapes. Descendants of Banquo found the Stewart dynasty of kings of Scotland, forefathers of king James.

Overcome by guilt and depression, Macbeth seeks additional prophesies. He is told no man born of woman will harm him unless Birnam Wood comes to Dunsinane. Knowing that all men are born of woman and that trees cannot walk, Macbeth is relieved.

The bloody treachery of Macbeth does not end once he is king. Macduff was a witness to the murder of Duncan, so Macbeth travels to Macduff's castle where he slays all found there, including Lady Macduff and her son. Macduff was not home. The stage is set for Macduff and Macbeth to meet in battle at Dunsinane Hill, coincidentally, the real-life location of the real Macbeth's battle with Duncan in 1054.

Unknown to Macbeth, Macduff was born in a crude caesarian procedure, not in natural childbirth. Macduff orders his men to cut branches from trees in Birnam Wood and creep forward holding camouflage. During the battle, Macduff slays Macbeth. Peace and reason are restored to Scotland when Macduff is crowned king of Scotland on the Stone at Scone.

Audiences at performances of *Macbeth* in 1606, Shakespeare's Scottish play, were not troubled by Macduff becoming king of Scotland, rather than a descendant of Banquo. Theatergoers were savvy to political facts of the day. Banquo's sons became king, of that they had proof. James VI of Scotland was crowned James I of England. The Stewart dynasty of English kings began. Shakespeare validated his new Scottish patron king.

## The Politics of History Retold

Casual readers of Shakespeare may ask why it was necessary to transform Macbeth from dutiful leader to bloody thug. Why must Shakespeare look to Scotland for a plot when he had success with escapades of English kings? The answers lie in politics and timing.

By 1599 William Shakespeare, formerly of Stratford-on-the-Avon, was a wealthy London playwright. He moved to a home on the banks of the Thames, near his popular theater, the Globe. His benefactor, Queen Elizabeth I, enjoyed his comedies. Comedies involved mistaken identity creating confusion in lives of lovely people, which were sorted out in the end. Tragedies, where everyone died in the end, were less popular with the queen.

Queen Elizabeth died in 1603. Shakespeare needed a new royal patron. Scottish King James VI became James I of England. James believed in the divine right of kings, although his new subjects in England were not convinced. Shakespeare seized on an opportunity to impress the new king. He renamed his company the King's Men and began work on a Scottish play, validating the right of James to rule by clarifying his lineage.

*Macbeth* was written from 1604 to 1606, first performed in 1606, and held for publication in 1623, at the end of Shakespeare's life. In 1604 James proposed union of Scotland and England, although the English were cool to the idea. Scots were regarded in England as unruly distant cousins. Scots determined succession of royals in battle, of which Macbeth was an example. Civilized English preferred royals ascending by inheritance.[40]

In the 15th and 16th centuries, Scottish Moray, homeland of the real Macbeth, was a lawless area of cattle thieves. Meanwhile, the Scottish crown moved peacefully through Duncan's lineage to his nephew Malcolm. Scottish and English royals intermarried. Malcolm III married the sainted Margaret of England. Margaret is Scotland's only royal saint.

English king Henry I married Edith, the daughter of Malcolm III. Their grandson was Henry II. In 1503, James IV of Scotland married Margaret Tudor, the sister of Henry VIII and the aunt of Queen Elizabeth I.

Shakespeare was not alone in inventing a pro-Stewart and anti-Macbeth story. He was informed by the *Chronicles of England, Scotland, and Ireland*, written in 1577 by Ralph Holinshed. Holinshed portrayed Macbeth as a murderous tyrant of the dark ages.[41]

---

[40] A century later, Parliament preferred Protestant German George I, rather than Catholic Scot, James VII and II.

[41] Holinshed had a reputation for accuracy. In Tales of a *Grandfather*, in 1827, Sir Walter Scott adopted Holinshed's portrait of Macbeth. Scott redeemed himself in 1829, in *History of Scotland*, with a factual description of Macbeth.

Shakespeare knew James VI and I was fascinated by witches.[42] Macbeth is the only Shakespeare play with scenes of witches. Evil deeds, shaped by supernatural forces was a theme in *Macbeth*. In 1611, James I proved his virtue, when he signed the *Magna Carta*.

*James I Signing the Magna Carta*

## Visiting Glamis Castle Today

In fields near Glamis are where the final battle of Malcolm II in 1034 occurred. Malcolm was taken to a hunting lodge, where he died. That lodge is at the foundation of present-day Glamis Castle. Guides say rooms are haunted by Malcolm's ghost. Duncan was murdered in his castle near Inverness, although Glamis Castle aficionados claim the murder also occurred at Glamis. A castle existed at Glamis since 1376. In 1540, the lady of Glamis Castle was burned as a witch on orders of James V, the father of Shakespeare's patron king. The castle seen today was erected in the 15th century, giving it centuries to acquire the historic patina that inspired Shakespeare to make it the venue for his play.

---

[42] Fiona Watson, Macbeth: A True Story, at 19.

# TAX COURT
## – WINCHESTER
### Domesday Book & Taxes of William I

*Great Hall of William's Law Court Winchester*

The story of modern England began when an insignificant outpost of the Roman Empire evolved into a nation, which produced and disseminated more ideas and institutions than any state since Athens.[43] The catalyst of change was William, Duke of Normandy, descendant of Norsemen, who settled in northern France and became Normans. William was known in his time as William the Bastard, or king William I, the Conqueror, depending on view of the scribe. There is no doubt that he established England's modern Parliament, which sits today on remnants of William's court.

Governments are built on funds of the governed. William was confident he could conquer turf, but he recognized that building a ruling infrastructure required steady, dependable income. The genius and legacy of William in forming a stable, powerful nation was in his scheme of taxation, rather than continual war to raid for wealth, to fund the government.

To efficiently collect taxes, William required knowledge of his subjects. In 1085, William ordered compilation of a Great Survey of taxable supplicants of the predecessor king Edward. Completed in 1086, the survey record is known as the Domesday Book.[44]

In a monarchy, there was no concern for enfranchisement of voters by land ownership. That came later in England, necessitating the 1873 book of landowners, regarded as a second Domesday Book. The second survey was instigated by lords of land, identifying extent of their domain, later regretted when used to tax land, income, and rents.

## The Great Survey of the Domesday Book

Monumental in scope, the Great Survey faced hurdles in definition of taxable estates. The task required defining responsibility for taxes in feudal society, when emerging urban trade fairs defied traditional means of income. Assessing farms for a percent of the crop, as a use tax, was an easy matter. Tennant

---

[43] Lacey Baldwin Smith, This Realm of England 2nd ed., Heath and Company, Lexington, 1971.
[44] The 1783 published edition is held in the National Archives at Kew. www.domesdaybook.co.uk

farmers gave a portion of their crop to feudal landlords, responsible to the king. All land was owned by the king.

In the feudal world inherited by William, acreage and herds of livestock were counted, not people. People were listed as tenants and subtenants, with various rights to retain valuable goods. As a census of England in the 11th century, the survey accounted for about a fifth to a sixth of the actual population. Families of farmers and millers were not counted. Slaves were counted as assets.

Either the English economy expanded in William's peacetime, or his scribes were more effective than those of predecessors in capturing the picture of wealth in England. The Domesday Book records over five thousand mills and a diversity of harvested resources, such as honey, and manufactured goods, such as metals used in minted coins.

It is interesting to note areas not included in the Great Survey. Portions of London and Winchester were omitted since these were lands of royals or clergy, exempt from taxes. Such exemptions continue today. Battle captains of William were given conquered border areas, also not taxed. Lords expended their own funds in defense of grants of turf.

Assessments due to the king extended beyond goods and crops. Lords and landlords-in-chief owed a specified number of soldiers for service in the king's army. Soldiers were fed and equipped as part of the assessment. If the military contingent was deficient in number, the debt was carried over to the next assessment.

So effective were the king's assessors in compiling the Domesday Book, that its veracity stood over time. Data from the book was admitted as evidence in court cases over the millennium. In the 21st century the Domesday Book was used to settle land disputes, shoreline access, and rights to hunt.

## William's Courts of Law

Law courts of William I were forums for validating tax records for the Domesday Book, rather than for resolution of rights or compensation for harms. Areas of England were recorded as shires, analogous to counties. In subsets of counties, townships sent representatives to present their case. The forums functioned as oral submission of tax reports, wherein taxpayers had an opportunity to minimize their assessment.

Reports of the king's tax assessors and pleas of taxpayers were heard in court by twelve jurors. William's law required six jurors who were Englishmen and six who were Norman. Normans were French speaking countrymen of the king, though less biased toward the king, as their local interests increased. Englishmen, not conversant in the business language of French, were at a disadvantage. They knew where to hide beer and cheese.

## The Odo Factor

William and his sister Adelaide were children of the beautiful commoner Herleva and her lover, the Duke of Normandy. In his will, the duke provided land to the gentleman who married Herleva. The couple had two more children: Robert and Odo.

Odo was a legitimate royal, devoted to William, aspiring only to a life in the church. Odo's devotion might have been brotherly love. More likely, Odo tied himself to the best candidate likely to rise to rule. He was not disappointed.

When William became the Duke of Normandy in 1035, Odo helped minimize political infighting. William repaid Odo with an appointment as the Bishop of Bayeux in 1049. Critics were enraged at the youth and inexperience of the new bishop. Odo was likely nineteen, although he looked as though he was fourteen. It was easy to dislike Odo.[45]

The Battle of Hastings in 1066 resolved title to the English crown in William and began a period of relative calm in England. William was forever defending his right to the throne from contenders in north England, while maintaining his Dukedom in Normandy. William spent a great deal of time in Normandy, leaving Odo to rule England.

---

[45] Andrew Bridgeford, *1066: The Hidden History in the Bayeux Tapestry*, Walter and Company, New York, 2004.

William made Odo the Earl of Kent, a wealthy area, which included Canterbury. Their other brother, Robert, remained in France. Robert was loyal to William, though neither was successful in containing antics of Odo.

William never learned to read. It was more important to be a knight. When he was twenty-four, William married Matilda and they had ten children. Giving England a healthy successor to the throne was important to William.

Odo is featured in the famous Bayeux Tapestry in positions of great authority that belie his peripheral involvement in events of the Battle of Hastings depicted in the tapestry. Odo takes center stage ordering shipbuilding. Ships are seen crossing the channel, loaded with horses and men. The arriving army has a meal, shown with similarity to the *Last Supper*, blessed by Bishop Odo. Next is a scene of the threesome, Odo, William, and Robert. It is uncontroverted that Odo received the tapestry, which hung periodically in his cathedral in Bayeux. Creator of the tapestry is a mystery.

Most historians attribute the tapestry to Odo.[46] They note the tapestry was created in England, probably Canterbury, within Odo's domain as the Earl of Kent. The tapestry adorned Odo's Bayeux church. Also, two young knights, protectors of Odo, who received lands from him in Kent, are identified in the tapestry. Their names, Wadard and Vital, appear in the tapestry, though they were not distinguished figures in events of 1066.

Tapestry historian, Carola Hicks, offers another theory.[47] Hicks identifies queen Edith, widow of king Edward, the sister of Harold vanquished at Hastings, as the logical choice for patron of the tapestry. As widow of the former king, she lost a great deal of authority. She backed the wrong horse in her brother's attempt at the throne. Three of her brothers died in the battle in 1066. She employed embroiderers in England. Hicks asserts Edith wanted to protect her assets. The way to secure herself, in the reign of King William, was an appeal to the man wielding the power of grace or retribution, Bishop Odo.

Odo was a flawed figure. Although a man of the church, he maintained a mistress and had a son. As brother to the king, and Earl of Kent, he took ownership of 184 manors, building one of the largest estates in British history.

---

[46] Eyewitness Travel, France, DK, London, 2006, at 252.
[47] Carola Hicks, The Bayeux Tapestry, Vintage Books, London, 2006.

In 2000, the British Sunday Times published a list of the richest non-royal Britons of all time. Odo ranked number four. His wealth at present value was £43.2 billion.[48] His assets are recorded in the Domesday Book.

Odo was never liked in France, where he became a bishop ahead of those who thought themselves more pious and deserving. Odo created problems for William in England, whenever William went to Normandy to protect his French turf. In 1067, while William was in Normandy, English nobles attacked Dover Castle, Odo's home in England. Odo was not there, but there was a considerable loss of life.

The downfall of Odo began in 1076, when the Archbishop of Canterbury disputed pre-conquest land owned by the archbishop, taken by Odo. Odo lost the case. Acrimony continued between the two clerics.

Undaunted by defeat in court, Odo launched a military expedition to Italy to be named pope. Unable to ignore antics of his brother, William had Odo imprisoned. Odo lost his title as earl and estates in Kent while in prison but managed to remain a bishop.

Once released from prison upon William's death in 1087, Odo began a rebellion to unseat his nephew, King William II. English subjects rallied for their new king. Lore has it that Odo under siege in Rochester Castle was hounded by a plague of flies in his escape.[49]

Odo found a home in Palermo, where he died in 1097. He donated heavily to the Palermo Cathedral, where he commissioned his tomb. Less than 100 years later the tomb was dismantled. Odo is now in a side chapel dedicated to Mary Magdalene.

# Law Court in Winchester

The Great Hall of William I in Winchester is now ensconced in the Winchester Combined Court Center. In an annual ceremony, gates in the historic hall open as new barristers flow from the 1970s building to William's Hall, with

---

[48] Bridgeford, at 210.
[49] King Henry I gave Odo's Rochester Castle to the Bishop of Canterbury. The castle has the highest Norman castle keep in England.

its 13th century Round Table. In 1973, trial of six IRA members was held here, charged with bombing the Old Bailey in London.

King Edward I (Edward Longshanks, not Edward Confessor) issued the Statute of Winchester in 1285. The law served as the policing ordinance until an 1829 law established metropolitan police. The law set times for closing city gates, required pursuit of robbers, and kept fairs and commercial activity off the church lawn. Over the centuries, William's law court evolved from tax court to civil justice. His methods still fund the government.

*Odo's Rochester Castle*

*Hanseatic Lighthouse Warnemünde*

# COMMERCIAL CODE –
## LÜBECK, WARNEMÜNDE, AND ROSTOCK

### The Hanseatic League

*Lübeck Town Square*

In northern German towns along the Baltic Sea, the glacial grip of medieval life melted away centuries before the Renaissance arrived in Italy. While 12th century petty dukes competed among themselves, democratic concepts grew in market centers and ports affording inland German cities access to the sea, notably Lübeck and Rostock. Secure in the inertia of tradition, nobles were surprised when shipbuilders, sailors, and merchants asserted independence by trade agreements. Medieval fiefs lost relevance and tax income.

What began as a practical arrangement to enable a small market economy, in the absence of overlords, evolved into an inter-port guild of seamen, merchants, and diplomats. At its height, the guild encompassed 170 cities.

Guilds asserted self-rule with elected councils, sent envoys to meetings, and negotiated treaties with world powers such as England.

In 1356, the guild gave itself a name, the Hanseatic League. League members pledged mutual support and defense. Instead of war to resolve differences they used consensus and compromise agreements. Rather than empty shops, mills, and industrial centers to provide soldiers to nobles, they purchased armies. The League protected its interests.

The Hanseatic League dominated trade on the Baltic Sea for centuries. Coincidental to the rise of the League was the demise of feudalism. Late in the 15$^{th}$ century, German nobles reasserted control. They could not revive feudalism.

Rostock and its port of Warnemünde are iconic of League towns. Initially founded by Slavs, Rostock grew as a Hanseatic League enterprise. In the 19$^{th}$ century, when the Hanseatic League ceased to exist, Rostock moved forward on its Hanseatic foundation. Rostock still refers to itself as a Hanseatic city: German, enterprising, and democratic.

This is the story of the Hanseatic League as it caused a quantum shift in human life and commerce. It is also the story of Hanseatic cities, of which Rostock is an example. Cruise ships port at Warnemünde. Visitors take a short train ride down the Warnow River to Rostock. In Rostock, as in Lübeck, Visby, Bergen and elsewhere Hansa evidence endures.

## Hanseatic Revolution – Development of International Commercial Code

Twelfth century Germany, like most of Europe, was locked in feudalism, where few nobles controlled the land, the people who worked the land, and the crops, timber, and products created within the domain of the overlord. Nobles had a habit of increasing holdings by war with neighbors. War only diminished their assets and population of workers. Within society there were few freeborn men, who had freedom of movement and the ability to engage in business. These non-royals owned ships instead of land.

Free men were involved in commerce, the movement of goods between domains of nobles. Foreigners were not welcome in ports of medieval royals. As traders expanded their reach, they were allowed stays of a few months, not more than three times in a year.

In 1159, Henry the Lion, the Duke of Saxony and Bavaria, in present day Germany, captured the town of Lübeck from royals and rebuilt it. His goal was having a port on the Baltic Sea from which to command trade between minor nobles. The modest goal of Henry was protecting his ships from pirates and Vikings, as he moved herring, cloth, and wood from interior towns to ports of Scandinavia.

Henry was a businessman, not a soldier, except when necessary. He was an opportunist, not a revolutionary. By his acts, Henry instigated an end to the medieval world order and the beginning of Lübeck as a center of Baltic and North Sea trade.

Over the next century, merchants from a growing number of ports of the Baltic and North Sea traded in hemp from Brugge to candle wax from Novgorod. In the 1220s, an over-winter trading station was established at Novgorod called Peterhof. Member merchants of guild houses referred to themselves as Hansa. Living quarters for traders were called Kontor. Kontors were free zones, under the control of no king.

Hansa Kontors opened in Lübeck, Rostock, Hamburg, Novgorod, Visby on Gotland Island, Danzig, the present-day Gdansk, Steelyard of London, Brugge, Tallinn, and Bergen. There were no agents or credit transactions. Not until late 15th century did Italian bankers invent credit instruments, double entry bookkeeping, and standardized coin.

Inland cities, such as Cologne prospered by bringing cloth and farm products to Lübeck, which shipped to world markets. Lübeck of Henry the Lion became the Queen of Hansa, a center of world trade. All Hansa towns benefited from trade.

The merchant class grew in power and wealth exceeding that of nobles. Merchants bought land from cash strapped nobles. When royals pressed Hansa towns for men to populate armies, Hansa sent payment in lieu of service. Eventually, Hansa towns formalized their relationship and employed their own army.

In 1356, Hansa towns held a convention. In the Diet of Hansa, they formalized relationships into the Hanseatic League. The League collected dues from members to pay armies for mutual defense. They pledged each other mutual aid. The Hansa code was known as the Law of Lübeck. It was the law of trade. Members were expected to live by the law or be expelled from the League. Re-entry for a town came at a steep price.

Benefits of League membership included defense against pirates and encroaching nobles. Lighthouses were built, ensuring safe harbors in League towns. The League built ships and opened new markets. Rostock had lucrative commissions to build League ships.

A council governed each League town. Town residents elected council members. League towns were free of constraints imposed in feudal society. Craftsmen flourished.

As testament to the strength of Hansa, agreements with kings were not reciprocal. The English king, for example, allowed duty-fee Hansa goods into England. The English prized wood from Danzig for crossbows, delivered on Hansa ships. Hansa merchants financed England's Black Prince in his victory at Crecy, France, joined by his friend, Geoffrey Chaucer. His father, Edward III, posted crown jewels as collateral on the loan.

From 1361 to 1370, the League went to war against Denmark for primacy in the Baltic. Copenhagen in Denmark and Helsingborg in Sweden were sacked. The king of Denmark, Valdemar IV, and the king of Norway, Håkon VI, were required to remit 15% of their profits from trade in the Baltic and North Sea to the League. The 1370 Treaty of Stralsund gave the Hanseatic League a trade monopoly in Scandinavia. Danes rebelled in 1426, resulting in another war. In the end, the earlier treaty was renewed in favor of Hansa.

A trade monopoly did not mean the League had total control of the seas. There were pirate problems. In 1392, Albert of Mecklenburg, king of Sweden, hired notorious pirates the Victual Brothers, to harass ships of his rival Margaret I, queen of Denmark. From a hideout in Visby, pirates captured vessels in the

Baltic. When Denmark and Sweden resolved their differences, the Victual Brothers focused on capture of Hansa ships.

Leader of the Victual Brothers was Klaus Störtebeker, whose name in Saxon means empty a beer stein in one gulp. When he was not downing quantities of ale, Störtebeker was capturing cargo, executing the crew, and sinking ships. His reign ended when Hansa sailor Simon, of Bergen, Norway, sailed close to the pirate ship and threw molten lead on the rudder chain. With his ship disabled, the pirate king was captured with forty crew. Some chronicles of 1400 reported hundreds of captured pirates. It was a big news item. All captured pirates were shortened by a head.

## Deflating Hansa

In the 15th century, the League faced powerful opposition. By 1438, the Dutch mastered international trade. Amsterdam, not a Hansa city, broke the Hansa monopoly by trading with England, Russia, and in Africa. In a three-year war, resolved in 1441, Hansa and the Dutch afforded each other space for commerce in the Baltic and North Seas.

By the end of the 15th century, nobles realized their squabbles enabled Hansa's power. Nobles of Germany and the Baltic joined in 1495, at a Diet of Worms, planning a return to power. On the agenda were reassertion of power, peace agreements between nobles, and collection of taxes. Topics were portrayed as government reforms.

Reform to Hansa cities meant continuing trade without royal interference. Taxes to the crown were paid in tons of herring. Hansa currency was smoked, salted, or pickled.

Also eroding dominance of the League in world trade by the end of the 15th century were Russia, Italy, and Poland. When Ivan the Terrible took power in 1494, he closed the Kontor at Novgorod. Italians expanded trade using credit instruments. A Genoese bank financed return voyages of Columbus to the New World. In 1466, Danzig began a century as part of the Kingdom of Poland. Loss of Danzig in the League was costly.

The Hanseatic League was a victim of its success. Vibrant, wealthy cities established separate militaries, or in joinder with rising powerful nation states. Cities negotiated trade agreements separate from the League. In 1597, Queen Elizabeth I expelled the League from London and closed Steelyard. One-sided agreements were not her style.

By 1669, there remained nine League members. At the final meeting in 1862, there were three cities: Lübeck, Hamburg, and Bremen. Bergen and Rostock, among others, still refer to themselves as Hanseatic League cities, as an historical connection to glory days.

Although the Hanseatic League is defunct, its legacy is visible in daily lives of former Hansa towns. The concept of rule by council owes its popularity to the League. Decision-making by consensus and compromise is still preferable to war to resolve differences. Use of envoys negotiating trade agreements creates prosperous economies for all involved.

## Iconic Hansa Rostock Rises

*Rostock Market Square*

In Slavic language, Rostock means at the fork of a river. The town was founded by Slavs in the 11th century at the mouth of the Warnow River and burned in 1161 by order of Danish king Valdemar I. A new Rostock rose from ashes in the 13th century as a Hanseatic League town, under Lübeck Law. In 1283, the Rostock Peace Treaty ensured the port growth as a mercantile center. By 1323, Rostock encompassed Warnemünde, a popular resort town.

Rostock in the Hansa era was graced by Brick-Gothic buildings, seen in the city today. Brick-Gothic employs creative use of simple bricks rather than ornate stone in municipal buildings. The University of Rostock was founded in 1419, a tribute to Hansa esteem.

Fortunes of Rostock coincided with the Hanseatic League. In the 16th century, when German royals instituted a tax on beer, revenue went to royals. The town suffered.

In a weakened state, Rostock began each of the next three centuries occupied by a foreign power. From 1618 to 1648, and from 1700 to 1721, Denmark and Sweden held the northern German coast, which included Rostock. In 1806, Napoleon rendered Rostock a French vassal city. During World War II, Rostock was heavily bombed by the Allies.

Today Rostock is restored as a Hansa city, in its Brick Gothic glory. Warnemünde is still a popular resort town. Lübeck is a favorite shore excursion. Hansa is a German sports team.

*Schwerin Castle Germany*

# LAND TITLE - GERMANY

## Schwabenspiegel Code of Fiefdoms

The Schwabenspiegel is a 13th century restatement of property law.[50] The Franciscan monk creating the opus work in 1275, in vernacular of Middle High German, rather than Latin, captured realities of feudalism without sympathy or entitlement. It is as it was.

A subtitle to the work is Mirror of the Swabians, also known as Saxons. Writing in Augsburg, thirty miles from the Saxon capital of Munich, the friar's effort was informed by the 1235 Sachsenspiegel, also in Middle High German, translated from Latin by a Saxon knight. Latin was the language of exclusivity in the Catholic church. Sachsenspiegel was a secular law code, beyond church doctrine.

Put in context of the times, Latin and dictates of the Catholic church centered in Rome were amid a Great Schism, beginning in the 10th century and coming to full fruition in the 15th century, with Eastern Orthodoxy splitting from the Vatican. For much of the 14th century, not even popes wanted to live in Rome, choosing instead the clear skies of Avignon. The bloody Reformation of the early 16th century, instigated in part by another Augsburg friar, Martin Luther, had not yet permeated monastic visions. Friars saw themselves as keepers of knowledge of religious and secular order. Writing in German rather than Latin was a bit of local conceit, not intended as a revolutionary act.

---

[50] This story relies in part, with gratitude, upon an English translation by William John Slayton, Master's Thesis, Rice University, 1967.

To friars of Augsburg, Germany was the center of civil law. Otto the Great, king of the Franks, predecessor to Germany, ruled a vast, well-organized empire. In 962 he dubbed himself the Holy Roman Emperor. Though seemingly religious title, the HRE was a political entity.[51] Otto offered subjects a secular, stable, powerful option to the pope.

The nameless author of Schwabenspiegel, imbued in tradition, recorded empirical reality, informed by cannon law. Drawing from accepted wisdom, abstaining from originality, the Schwabenspiegel is a code incorporating earlier code, explained by cannon law and the Pentateuch, that is the first five books of Jewish law, the Old Testament of the Bible. Thus, Schwabenspiegel is the first Restatement of Property Law second edition.

Regarded today as a gem of medieval prose, the Schwabenspiegel author avoided literary criticism by grounding the text on higher, biblical authority. The code text was offered as preservation of laws faithfully transmitted orally over generations. Its veracity was solid.

## Schwabenspiegel – Restatement of Property 2$^{nd}$

Schwabenspiegel has two parts, encompassing territorial and feudal law. In feudal life of medieval times, people turned from tribal chiefs as fonts of authority, to land barons on whose turf they toiled. Tribes defined family not bounded by land. Kings ruled terrain, not bounded by family units. Wars were fought over land dominance of a ruling family. Resident vassals went with the land to the victor. Schwabenspiegal defined territorial authority and hierarchy.

Schwabenspiegel aimed for universal appeal. The Sachsenspiegel was a code of northern Germany. Just prior to the Schwabenspiegal, another Augsburg author produced the Deutshenspiegel relevant to southern Germany. Deutshenspiegel was quickly eclipsed. Schwabenspiegel became Kaiserrecht, that is, imperial law of the Holy Roman Empire.

---

[51] The HRE supplanted fractious tribal law. Slayton, at iv. The emperor's authority derived from Roman emperors, elected, usually Franks. At its height in the 12th century, the Empire included much of central Europe, northern Italy, Corsica, and Sardinia. It ended in 1806, a casualty of Napoleon's reorganization of medieval royal Europe.

In feudal society not all vassals were serfs, peasants, or slaves. Freemen as vassals to a lord looked to the lord for protection, just as the lord depended upon services of vassals in furtherance of the royal estate. Feudal hierarchy denoted privilege and function as well as reciprocal responsibility. Vassals in control of large fiefs owned by the lord could amass great wealth. Schwabenspiegel acknowledged inheritable use title to land in vassals.

By the 13th century, reciprocal needs of lords and vassals gave vassals bargaining power, leading to varied contractual arrangements. Nuanced property rights took shape. Obligations of parties were specified. Engagement of a vassal to manage a fief could be renounced by a vassal if the lord abused power or reneged on compensation. Rights of inheritance were express. Absent inheritance right to land, the fief reverted to the lord upon death of the occupant with use rights. Rights to sublet were also express.

Schwabenspiegel as a Book of Feudal Law begins with hierarchy in society. There are five levels of knights or royals, of which the king is number one. All rights vest from the king. Sixth in status are clergy. The seventh category is everyone else, those with rights not automatic by birth or title. The seventh category required clarification of rights in law.

Lawyers will appreciate that Schwabenspiegel addressed the Rule of Perpetuities. Forever is defined from Adam, through Noah, Abraham, and Moses, to Jesus Christ. Only the lord knows when the world will end. Until then, rights persist for a thousand years. (Book 1.b.)

Schwabenspiegel grants land in fee-title in the Law of the Seventh Hand. Lords may assign use rights six times. Upon the seventh assignment, transfer grants title. (Book 47).

Ladies have the same rights as clergy. They may inherit and transfer fee by inheritance. Their land rights survive a change of king. Land without heirs reverts to the king. (Book 4). A wife can inherit from her husband if male children do not object. (Book 60).

Vassals lumped in one level of the hierarchy have varied rights and receive much attention in the Schwabenspiegel. In an age of oral agreements, or oaths, process for establishing property rights required simple clarity. Vassals swear an oath of fealty to their lord, establishing obligations to serve in their best interests. A vassal may renounce a fief at any time without cause. Lords may only seize a fief from a vassal with cause. Just cause includes *fluthtsal*, refusal of a vassal to pay a creditor. (Book 105)

Vassals are excused from obligations to a lord who borrows a horse until it is returned. A vassal holding a fief for a year and a day has *right of possession*, if supported by two witnesses in good standing. A vassal asserting rights has the burden to give proof. (Book 6-7, 10-12). If claims of vassal and lord are deemed equal, the vassal wins. (Book 74).

Schwabenspiegel describes possible conflicts arising from claims of multiple vassals to a single fief. A forgetful lord might double endow. Oaths, timing, and witnesses were important. Kings had incentive to clarify from whom to expect rents and military service.

Military service was required of all nobles and vassals called by the king. Vassals served at their expense. No court actions, property or civil, could be taken against a soldier during service, or for six weeks after return. Military service was avoided by payment to the king. (Book 8). Ladies and clergy did not serve. They paid a war tax. (Book 68).

Court hearings always began by noon. Court was not held on holy days or days of rest. Hearings were held in the open, not in the lord's castle. (Book 115, 146). No armaments or armies of the lord were allowed at a court hearing. (Book 117).

By Schwabenspiegel rule, in an action of a lord asserting judgement on a vassal, there must be twelve vassals present, seven of whom must agree on a verdict. If the lord is not pleased, he can ask twenty more vassals to review the matter. Appeal is to the next highest lord and then to the king. No lord may take property from a vassal by force.

Only those holding property of value, not banished, or hiding from the law may give testimony in court. Vassals are to be assigned an advocate by the lord, approved by the vassal. (Book 9, 18-26, 36-37, 70). A vassal may forfeit a fief for failure to appear in court after twice receiving summons. (Book 82). A lord may not avoid a hearing by locking themselves in a castle. (Book 88).

When a fief holder dies leaving a pregnant wife, the fief will not revert to the lord when a son is born. Witness to a live birth must be by two ladies attending the birth. (Book 38).

Schwabenspiegel is comprehensive in remedies, including restitution due a lord or vassal, with disputed income held in trust until resolution, and rights of vassals when multiple lords appear. Lords owe vassals defense of the fief. Vassals have rights to accurate description of fief size and are allowed time to explore domain for accuracy. (Book 27-33). Vassals observing problems must complain timely or waive rights. (Book 35).

Secular power of bishops is affirmed in Schwabenspiegel. Church land was assigned in fee to the bishop, who could mint coins, collect taxes, and appoint judges in secular court. Judges sitting without authority, passing a death sentence, were subject to having their tongue cut out. Tongues were redeemable for a price. (Book 41).

Unlike succession of the throne, absent a will, fiefs did not automatically transfer to the oldest son. Children had an ability to decide among them the heir. Fiefs were not divisible, although brothers could jointly hold. (Book 56-58, 61).

## Legacy in Property Law

Many legal concepts described in Schwabenspiegel are recognized today. Giving notice, a twelve-person jury of whom seven must agree in civil cases, waiver of rights for failing to contest open possession of property by another, competent witnesses, burden of proof on the party asserting rights, and right of possession by contract, are legacies of Schwabenspiegel. It is today, as it was in Schwabenspiegel, military personnel may not have actions against them during pendency of active service. Youths require a guardian to administer property rights until age twenty-one. (Book 48 b). A witness must be eighteen.

Today 350 manuscripts of Schwabenspiegel exist, evidence of its broad appeal. It was afforded authority as gospel and statutory law, a winning combination. Contemporary translations in Latin, French, and Czech covered trade domains of the HRE. French law texts of the following century were largely informed by Schwabenspiegel. Several German lawbooks followed in the next century, falling short in attempts at improvement.

Author of Sachsenspiegel, the knight Eike von Repgow, turned from writing a collection of laws to a compellation of major historic events of the world since the Creation. Notable as prose, the task was overwhelming. The author of Schwabenspiegel may have instigated Eike's effort by writing a concise history of the world from the Old Testament, skipping to history of the Roman Empire, and ending with the Roman/German Holy Roman Empire. Schwabenspiegel put into historic context, established validity of the law and ruler.

Schwabenspiegel ends with a warning. Souls are condemned before God if they, *read it to foolish and ignorant people*, who will not understand the law. *It is good to read this book aloud to people who are intelligent*, as they will not alter its meaning. Note it well.

# CORPORATE SECURITIES – AMSTERDAM

## The Dutch East India Company

*Dutch East India Company VOC Amsterdam*

The 17th century was a Golden Age of world commerce for the Dutch. In one century, Amsterdam went from fishing hamlet to center of world trade. Income financed expansion of canals. When dominance ended, a vibrant commercial center remained.

In 1594 a small group of Amsterdam merchants joined in a bold effort to compete with Portuguese merchants holding a monopoly on spice trade in the Far East. The Dutch single-venture Far Lands Company had mixed success. It proved the Dutch were capable of competing, much to delight of Asian suppliers, who raised prices for goods.

Sensing lucrative possibilities, Prince Mauritus, of United Provinces of the Netherlands, chartered a single company, with immense powers, forcing joinder of Amsterdam merchants. In 1602, the Verenigde Oostindische Compagnie, or VOC, known as the Dutch East India Company, became the world's first investor-owned public corporation. The VOC fulfilled grand dreams of the prince and his new nobles, investors of Amsterdam.

By the time war and competition with replicators of the DEIC in England and France clipped profits of the VOC in 1672, it established a vast trading network. The Dutch looked to the West Indies in a second iteration as the Dutch West India Company. The VOC established outposts, which became cities. Dutch investors became wealthy.

The VOC was the first private, world corporation, with a governing board, stockholders, and a multi-national network able to monopolize world trade in the most desirable goods on the European market. Kings still ruled countries as they did in the past. Commercial corporations were rulers of the world. This is the VOC story.

## From Spanish Vassal to World Leader

Great ideas altering government function do not materialize in a vacuum. Neither does a non-strategic city become an epicenter of world trade without a catalyst. Events coinciding in late 16$^{th}$ century Amsterdam fostered action. They were departure of Catholic Philip II of Spain from power over the Dutch region; migration of Protestants to Holland, the northern provinces of former Spanish Lowlands seeking religious freedom; and greed of Portuguese merchants, who raised costs of spices beyond Dutch toleration.

In 1567 Philip II became king of Spain and inherited the Spanish Lowlands, which included seven Dutch Provinces in the north, a divided Flemish and Walloon Belgium in the south, and Luxemburg. The north was predominantly Protestant, and the south was predominantly Catholic. Philip was an ardent Catholic, intolerant of Dutch Calvinists.

William the Duke of Orange, champion of the Dutch, led revolt in 1572. Hostilities resolved in the 1579 Treaty of Utrecht, in which the north achieved independence from Philip and remained Protestant, while the south stayed under Catholic Philip. Amsterdam prospered, overtaking Antwerp as a leading North Sea commercial port.

Protestants in Antwerp moved to Amsterdam. Their cash infusion to ship building in Amsterdam was accompanied by arrival of talented craftsmen and veterans of Far East trade with Portuguese merchants. Capital, skill, and experience merged in Amsterdam.

## The Dutch East India Company

Ships left Amsterdam in 1595 loaded with gold and trinkets to trade for pepper in Java, now Indonesian Islands. Dutch rulers blessed the venture by waiving duties on expected imports. Despite experienced captains, it was a naïve endeavor.

Captains quarreled, turning a journey of several months into a 15-month ordeal. Once in Java there were no diplomatic relations facilitating trade. By the time ships returned to Amsterdam, pepper profits barely covered costs of the venture.

The governor of United Dutch Provinces realized factions must unite. In 1602, he gave a twenty-year charter to Verenigde Oostindische Compagnie, VOC, known in English as Dutch East India Company (DEIC).

The DEIC had exclusive, renewable, trade rights in the Far East. It had power to make treaties on behalf of the Dutch government, enlist soldiers, and wage war. The Company established trading posts on foreign soil, built forts to protect Dutch interests, including warehouses, and placed administrators in foreign ports, functioning as local governors.

Independent merchant consortiums joined the DEIC. Directors of former companies were directors of the DEIC and major stockholders. Anyone could buy stock in VOC. The board directed operations, hired employees, and chose time and place of goods auctions.

Directors each received 1% of DEIC net income. Later, directors received 3000 guilders a year, plus travel expenses. All shareholders received lucrative returns. The number of shares was fixed and never diluted. If the DEIC required capital for building ships and purchasing gold for minting coins, they obtained loans. Creditors were paid from proceeds and had first choice in purchases. In a pinch, the government provided loans.

Investors in the DEIC were wealthy merchants, ordinary wage earners, and clergy. All became wealthy on DEIC earnings. Over the 200-year DEIC lifetime, return on investment was 3600%.[52] There were 230 million guilders in annual transactions when yearly income of tradesmen was 300 guilders and Rembrandt charged 500 guilders for a portrait. At its height, capitalization of the DEIC on deposit was 6.5 million guilders.

DEIC sailed to Jakarta, Ceylon, and India. Ships returned with pepper, other spices, silk, other textiles, tea, and sugar. To facilitate shipping goods, stations were established at the Cape of Good Hope near Cape Town, Cape Verde, St. Helena, and Madagascar.

The VOC employed experienced master seamen. They hired talented mapmakers and held navigational maps in secret vaults in the East India House in Amsterdam. Maps were never printed on presses. They were copied on velum to preserve the ink and minimize proliferation of proprietary information.

The VOC sent envoys to Indonesia, India, Ceylon, and Japan to negotiate favorable trade status. When local growers refused to give the Dutch preferential treatment, the VOC landed troops to enforce trade monopolies. The Japanese gave the Dutch a monopoly in trade from 1641 to 1853. During this time, Japanese silk kimonos were a popular fashion staple in Amsterdam. In Batavia, present day Jakarta, of 140,000 inhabitants of the city in 1619, 6,000 were European merchants and 1200 were VOC soldiers.[53]

In 1621 the VOC founded the Dutch West India Company. Once again, impetus was competition with the Portuguese for trade and resources, this

---

[52] Els M. Jacobs, In Pursuit of Pepper and Tea, Netherlands Maritime Museum, Amsterdam, 1991, at 16.
[53] Jacobs, at 76.

time in the New World. The VOC established colonies in Sint Maarten, desired for salt ponds. Southern Caribbean islands of Aruba, Bonaire, and Curacao became Netherlands Antilles, a source of salt and fresh water. In 1634, VOC built a fort on Curacao to protect goods in transit from Suriname sugar plantations.

Dutch merchant Peter Stuyvesant was a director of the Dutch West India Company managing company operations in Curacao from 1642 to 1644. In 1644, Stuyvesant lost a leg in battle ousting Spanish troops from Sint Maarten. Legend has it that he sent the leg to Curacao for burial before he went to Holland to convalesce.

In 1647, Stuyvesant went to New Amsterdam for the VOC. He ruled the territory until English King Charles II granted the land to his brother, the Duke of York, eventually King James II. The action prompted a third Anglo-Dutch War. Wars depleted VOC funds. Stuyvesant capitulated in transfer of New Amsterdam to England in 1664, becoming New York. VOC held possessions in the Caribbean, Netherlands Antilles, and Suriname.

## Golden Age of Amsterdam to Exit of the VOC and a New Dutch Era

The VOC was the largest employer in Amsterdam, engaging 1000 workers in the city by the 18th century. Wages were high. Key employees received a home and free beer. Building VOC ships in Amsterdam, provisioning ships, and handling export and import at city docks fueled prosperity in the city. The VOC built 1500 ships over 200 years, most in the 17th century. The launch of a new ship was a major city event.

Toward the end of the 18th century, larger and longer ships with greater capacity were built. Early ships were square-riggers, dependent upon direction of the wind for travel. Newer ships used several masts of sails to harness the wind.

Amsterdam, flush with wealth, repaired dikes, built more ring canals, and reclaimed land at the harbor, resulting in the streetscape seen today. Merchants built lovely homes on the new canals. Talent flocked to the city. Rembrandt arrived to stay in 1631.

In the 17th and 18th centuries VOC was the largest shipping company in the world. For a Dutchman, holding VOC stock was as prized as a Rembrandt portrait. By the end of the 18th century VOC was bankrupt. A Fourth Anglo-Dutch War drained company funds. During the war trade was suspended. VOC defaulted on loans and reduced workers.

In Jakarta, plantation slaves revolted against onerous working conditions. Stockholders in Amsterdam, general folk not involved in VOC operations, were horrified learning wealth grew from slavery. They divested VOC stock. In 1795, Napoleon invaded the Dutch Republic. VOC access to government loans halted. The French liquidated VOC assets.

After the Napoleonic war, Dutch international trade was absorbed by private Dutch enterprises. Amsterdam maintained though it did not grow. Holland became part of the Netherlands in the age of nations. The Dutch were among the last to abolish slavery, doing so in 1863. In 1901 the Dutch instituted an Ethical Policy, aimed at overcoming long-term effects of slavery in the Dutch Overseas Colonies.

Amsterdam attracts millions of visitors each year to the city preserved from VOC days. Visitors on cruise ships and river boats dock next to the VOC warehouse, where a replica VOC ship sits at anchor. The Amsterdam stock exchange building sits on a quiet plaza, often overlooked by visitors. Now just another of hundreds of historic city sites, these structures were power centers of world trade. Today Amsterdam is a favorite cruise port for its historic and cultural attractions. People enjoy the city the VOC built.

# DEBTORS & BANKRUPTCY – AMSTERDAM

## Tulip Envy to Tulip Frenzy

*Tulip Sellers on an Amsterdam Canal*

Universal symbols of love, celebration, and holiday cheer are flowers, such as tulips, chocolate, and diamonds. Nowhere in the world are these symbols joined more eloquently than in Amsterdam. This Dutch city was not the origination point for any of the three. It was when they arrived in Amsterdam that each was made more wonderful and desirable, until they became synonymous with the Dutch.

Chocolate came to Amsterdam in VOC ships as a durable, not tasty commodity. Local chocolatiers transformed the greasy harsh paste into roasted dark chocolate, soluble in water or milk, and when combined with sugar and formed into tempting shapes, demand for Dutch chocolate rivaled all other commodities in trade. Diamond cutting prowess came to Amsterdam with Portuguese Jews fleeing the Spanish/Portuguese Inquisition in the 15th through 18th centuries. Excluded from other Dutch guilds, Jews formed diamond cutting guilds, creating a new market item for which Amsterdam became famous. Chocolate and diamonds have their own stories.

Tulips originated in the wild east of the Black Sea. Ancient traders took bulbs to China. The first use of tulips in gardens was in Turkey. Sultans enjoyed masses of color.

When tulips came to Amsterdam in the 16th century, excitement over the flower reached a crescendo. The craze is known as *Tulipomania*, a time when the otherwise cautious Dutch gave into a penchant for gambling. Lovely little flowers were the cause of leveraged purchase agreements, structured ownership cartels, and review of Dutch bankruptcy laws. Mania for tulips cooled, although passion for growing tulips endures.

This is a short story of tulips, brought to glory and infamy in Amsterdam. Although Dutch tulips can be found at home, it is most enjoyable to experience them at the source. Heighten your appreciation for the lovely flowers by knowing their colorful past.

## A Short History of Tulips

Earliest known species of tulips came from the Caucasus area, east of the Black Sea. Grown in the wild, bulbs and flowers were small and not notable. Traders brought bulbs to south China where growth and proliferation was never robust. Tulips need winter.

As Ottoman Turks rode west in the 13th century, their tulip bulbs traveled well. When they conquered Constantinople in 1453 and made it their capital of Istanbul, bulbs were planted prominently in gardens of Topaki Palace. By 1520, Suleiman the Magnificent enjoyed 1500 varieties of cultivated tulips, favoring the long, pointed petals of russet and bright yellow. By 1630 there were eighty flower shops in Istanbul offering tulips.[54]

Credit for introducing tulips to Europe goes to Portuguese trader, Lopo Vaz de Sampayo. In his travels, Vaz saw tulips in Ceylon. Over the two years it took Vaz to reach Europe, tulip bulbs remained healthy enough to produce flowers when eventually planted.

Preferred cargo of the Dutch was spice and textiles. Bulbs were thought a novelty, or a strange onion, perhaps good to eat, but with little promise of profit. Late in the 16th century, yellow tulips popped up in gardens across Europe as botanists shared bulbs.

In 1559 a tulip was recorded in a Bavaria. Tulip blooms were seen in England in 1582 and in France in 1598. Most important to history were bulbs reaching the Netherlands by 1570.

Bulbs reaching the Netherlands came to Carolus Clusius, a great 16th century botanist. Clusius was born Charles de L'Escluse in France in 1526. Educated in Latin, Greek, and Flemish, Clusius traveled the Spanish Lowlands, as the Netherlands, Belgium, and Luxembourg were then known, always looking for unique plants. When it was expedient for Lutherans to leave France, Clusius Latinized his name and moved to Amsterdam.

Clusius wrote 4,000 letters to other botanists while he studied tulip bulbs. The question he pondered was whether plants should be groomed as flowers or a food item. Fortunately, the verdict was in favor of flowers.

In 1592 Clusius was appointed a botany professor at the University of Leiden, where he planted a large garden. So often did plant thieves remove tulips that Clusius threatened to give away remaining bulbs. He died in 1609 never knowing the legacy of his life's work.

In his opus work, *Historia*, Clusius recorded thirty-four tulip species, grouped into early, mid, and late-blooming varieties. Dutch botanists soon expanded tulip species to 120. By the 1630s of 1600 species of tulips catalogued, 500 were Dutch.

---

[54] See, Mike Dash, Tulipomania, Three Rivers Press, New York, 1999, at 21.

In the Netherlands, tulips were bred into yellow, red, pink, and white. Variations in color, such as red or pink combined with white, caused excitement among tulip enthusiasts. Soon unicolor tulips were sold in bulk, while connoisseurs prized tulips of varied color.

In 1608 a tulip-crazed miller traded his mill for a tulip. Higher prices for variegated color tulips were justified by rarity. Mother tulips produced few healthy offshoots, fostering scarcity of desired plants. Early in the 17th century, it was thought the prized condition resulted from aphids in bulbs, not a virus spread by aphids. Growers placed bulbs in a mound of aphids, producing only a feeding frenzy for bugs, not a desired result for bulbs.

Many residents in 1630s Netherlands had discretionary funds to purchase bulbs and plant gardens. Amsterdam was a major port for shipbuilding and goods for sale by the VOC. Work was plentiful and wages were rising. In 1631 Rembrandt van Rijn came from Leiden to Amsterdam to paint in the vibrant city of able patrons.

Rembrandt did not paint tulips. He painted aficionados of tulips such as Dr. Claes Pietersz, who was so fond of tulips that he changed his name to Dr. Nicolaes Tulip, or Tulp in Dutch. *The Anatomy Lesson of Dr. Nicolaes Tulp*, painted by Rembrandt in 1632, established the artist among Amsterdam society. Other artists painted tulips.

In 1630 a tradesman in Amsterdam earned about 300 guilders a year, enough to keep a small family clothed and fed. Tradesmen rarely owned property. In 1636 a weaver made 60,000 guilders in four months from astute trading in rare tulips.[55] When word spread in taverns of quick fortunes made from tulips, workingmen sold their tools for tulips.

Breeding tulips is slow work. A mother-bulb creates two or three baby bulbs in a year, for two or three years. Harvesting tulip seeds from a flower takes time and skill. Tulips grown from seed do not produce flowering bulbs for several years. Slow growth of tulip inventory fueled demand, until bulbs sold several times in a year for increasing prices.

---

[55] Dash, at 145.

The Dutch government never sanctioned tulip sales at auction. Sales were conducted in taverns after consumption of generous amounts of beer. As frenzy for tulips grew into mania, tulip connoisseurs of wealth collected rare bulbs. Tradesmen and laborers took risks on becoming instantly wealthy from tulips.

*Tulipomania*, as it was known, would not have devastated so many working people, but for leveraged purchases obtained with private loans, guaranteed on personal collateral. Enterprising sellers devised sales of futures, purchased with promissory notes, on bulbs not yet bloomed or not yet producing offshoots. Offshoots were sold, and resold, while still in the ground before blooming. Investments were a gamble at best.

It is often said of the Dutch that despite Calvinist moralism and restraint, they like to gamble. Tulip auctions preyed on gamblers' mentally, with hopes of quick wealth. In 1633 a house sold for three tulip bulbs. In 1636 bulb prices doubled in a week. At the height of mania, from December 1636 to February 5, 1637, 10 million guilders changed hands in one Dutch town. One red and white, highly prized Semper Augustus sold for 1,000 guilders and resold a month later for 10,000 guilders. On February 5, 1637, a bulb sold in a tavern for 5,200 guilders. The most Rembrandt received for a painting was 2,400 guilders.

Within a week of the February 5 auction there were no buyers in taverns. Word spread of few buyers and sellers panicked. Those left holding futures and pieces of syndicates in a single bulb realized they had no intrinsic value. Buyers defaulted on loans. Defaults radiated down the paper trail of creative purchasing schemes. Sacks of yellow or red bulbs had minimal value. Dutch debtors went to prison in 1637. Households lost everything.

The Dutch government never sanctioned bulb auctions. Futures trading was illegal. Defaulting Dutch florists looked to governments to save them from incarceration. Local governments looked to the Hague for a solution. The Hague passed the problem back to cities. Bankrupt traders blamed Jews and Mennonites, not part of sales, as scapegoats.

Reputable tulip collectors chided florists for irresponsible actions. Tulips fell from favor as gifts and were uprooted from gardens. Dr. Tulp took down his tulip adorned office sign.

In the end, everyone looked to courts for resolution. Tavern auctions were recorded on chalkboards, leaving no tangible evidence. Finally, cases were settled privately for 10% of debt value. Holders of bulbs consolidated holdings, becoming the beginnings of the new, smaller, restrained, and eventually highly successful tulip industry in the Netherlands.

By the 18th century a dozen tulip growers dominated Dutch tulip trade, most in Holland. Tulip growers learned to breed variegated tulips, not dependent upon disease for variation. Tulip varieties are grown year around making tulips available for all holidays.

## Tulips in Amsterdam Today

Today nine billion tulip bulbs are harvested annually in the Netherlands, most in Holland. Holland provides two-thirds of the world supply of tulips to florists. Peak season for viewing tulips in fields from Haarlem to Leiden is mid-April. Tulip sales rival in the Amsterdam economy with tulip tourists. Cruise guests arriving too early for tulips are treated to crocus and daffodil blooms and those who arrive late enjoy fields of lilies. South of Amsterdam is Aalsmeer, where billions of cut flowers and plants are sold at the largest flower auction in the world. Sales are recorded.

The Dutch no longer jail people for debt. Tulips are purchased from growers or retailers for immediate tender of the purchase amount. Investment risk is spread across fields of flowers. Prizes not houses are given for outstanding specimen. Life is serene and stable.

Amsterdam is a popular cruise port for the beauty of its streets and the depth of history easily accessed from the port. Ride a bicycle through streets, past chocolate shops and diamond factories then into low-lying, flower-filled country, as the Dutch love to do, or walk, or take a Pedi-cab. This is a gem of a city, in a small country, which has given the world means to mark meaningful moments in life with flowers, chocolate, and diamonds.

# BANKING & SECURITIES REGULATION – LORIENT

## Banking, John Law & French Stockholders

*Lorient in 1800 (public domain)*

In the 17th century, sailing captains mastered trade winds, traveling the globe seeking commercial ventures. While England, Portugal, and the Dutch established colonies and far-flung trade stations, French corsairs trolled the English Channel seeking easy targets among ships of other nations returning from Africa and India. Other Frenchmen built fleets and trade relations. By the middle of the 17th century, France entered the global trade race, with its own shareholder venture.

French entrepreneurs realized they did not need to be kings to live like kings. The objective of trade wars was financial gain, not conquest of land. Kings declared war. Entrepreneurs declared profit. Kings were only relevant as investors. France entered the new word of trade with the royally sanctioned French East India Company in 1664.

Two iterations of the French East India Company, the subject of this story, began with funding and protection from the government. Kings were Louis XIV and Louis XVI. Before Louis lost his head at the Bastille in 1789, he already lost his purse.

This is the story of the largest corporate collapse and French scandal of the 18th century. It has attributes of 20th century corporate implosions. Corporate directors grew in number and prioritized personal income over producing revenue. They acknowledged no responsibility to shareholders, employees, and contract holders. Capital to resolve the mess, not supplied by corporate owners, was sought from the government and public.

The French foray into international trade as the French East India Company began in Lorient. Lorient did not exist until built to suit the FEIC. The new port was a venue for this story of greed and mismanagement, leaving the word *bank* shunned in France.

# Rise of Lorient and French World Trade

Today Lorient is a cruise port and naval station. It began as a secondary port to Port Louis across the bay. Port Louis was for centuries home to fishermen and single ship merchants. It was a haven for French corsairs needing a friendly harbor. Spain built a fort in French Port Louis in the 16th century. By 1664, the port was insufficient to suit new ships.

Founders of the French East India Company snubbed Port Louis, preferring a new facility. Big, new warehouses were all in Lorient. Port Louis remained home to fishermen.

Then as now, India was a center of world trade. Portuguese traders established stations in India in the 16th century. England established trade with India in 1600. The Dutch East India Company began in 1602, and the Danish East India Company began in 1616.

French merchants traveled to India in 1603, for King Henri IV. Nothing much came of the venture with few ships and little capital. Imported gems and spices impressed Parisians.

Key to successful ventures were established supply stations and trade relationships. Ships did not go to one port to receive goods and return home. Rather, merchant ships ported on the way to and from the Far East collecting and selling goods. They made profit in each transaction. French customers paying high prices for spices, tea, and silk were desirous of eliminating foreign middlemen. French kings and merchants wanted to supply France with imports and reap their own profits from international commerce.

Early in the 17$^{th}$ century, warehouses in Lorient held goods of English or Dutch merchants. Lacking a French merchant marine, the French king gave Letters of Marque to corsairs, otherwise regarded as pirates, looting ships close to home. Glamorous corsairs shared loot with the king but did not afford France international trade.

The French were not absent from foreign trade voyages. Individual investors staked ships leaving France for China, India, and Madagascar. Achieving sustained trade was difficult. One ship lost in a storm could bankrupt investors. The French needed a unified company for investors building a fleet of ships, spreading risk, and enabling sustainable ventures.

## Politics of the Free Market and the First French East India Company

In 1664, Jean Baptiste Colbert pressed a friend to publish the pamphlet, *Politics of the Free Market*. The document was a manifesto for the French East India Company. Colbert was minister of finance for King Louis XIV. Louis XIV was known as the *Sun King*, a master of ballet and limitless extravagance. Keeping France solvent during spending sprees of Louis, and forestalling peasant revolt, required a brilliant financial mind.

Colbert believed government depended upon wealth of the state. His fiscal policies are known as *Colbertisms*.[56] Central to *Colbertism* was expansion of commerce in a favorable balance of trade. Colbert fostered charter companies for exports and imports, set up chambers of commerce, instituted protective tariffs and import duties, and founded the French merchant marine. His rules blocked foreign trade in French colonies.

Trade within France was a small matter to Colbert, best left to local guilds and tradesmen. The king taxed local endeavors, except those of the gentry and clergy. Foreign trade in wine and crops was controlled by the king, netting royal profit.

Bringing goods to a wide domestic market required a national transportation network. Since roads benefited locals, Colbert urged the king build roads with induced peasant *volunteer* labor. Louis seemed not to notice his drop in popularity. Roadbuilding burdened farmers, reducing capacity to supply cash crops. *Colbertism*, good in concept, caused implosion of the domestic economy.

Colbert cast Dutch competitors in the world marketplace as evil. If local merchants felt a financial pinch, Colbert blamed the Dutch. Goods obtained by the Dutch in the East Indies, such as sugar and tobacco, went through several markets, each taxed as imports, and repackaged multiple times before reaching France as high-priced commodities.

In 1664, Colbert encouraged people of Marseilles to build ships and trade at sea. He promised subsidy by the crown based on tonnage of merchandise imported or exported. His thought was any trade, local or import/export, increased taxes for the king.

Urged by Colbert, in 1664 King Louis XIV financed one-fifth of an East India Company. Remaining shares quickly sold to courtiers anxious to impress the King. The new company merged existing independent companies under the French banner.

---

[56] See mtholyoke.edu/acad/intrel/Colbert; newschool.edu/het//profiles/Colbert; Modern History Sourcebook: Jean-Baptiste Colbert (1619-1683): Memorandum on Trade, 1664, http://www.fordham.edu/halsall/mod/1664colbert.html.

The new company was short on ships and effective leadership, even though Colbert recruited François Caron, a thirty-year Dutch East India Company veteran as director. As Caron's assistant, Colbert chose Marcara Avanchintz, an Armenian trader from Persia. Caron and Avanchintz did not get along. In 1668, with a ship full of sugar and textiles, Caron put Avanchintz in leg irons, then dumped him in Madagascar.[57]

Unlike the British or Dutch East India companies, which were private commercial ventures, the French East India Company remained under the crown, with a fifty-year monopoly. From inception, there were differences of direction from the king as a major investor and directors. The king was fixated on having a settlement in Madagascar, while directors prioritized cargo and profits. Disparate priorities doomed the young company.

The initial French Madagascar venture ended with ships lost or wrecked. The only returning ship collected leather, ebony, pepper, amber, tobacco, and gold, without docking in Madagascar. In 1671, the king arrested the French crown governor of Madagascar for failing to establish a thriving settlement. He died in prison.

The replacement Madagascar governor took the settlement from unstable to worse. Remaining colonists abandoned Fort Dauphin by 1674, after conflict with locals when Frenchmen dumped Malagasy wives for newly arrived French women, mortally insulting locals.[58] By 1675, the settlement was in ashes.

FEIC directors were no better than the king in managing assets. Directors built a new port of Lorient, while maintaining offices in Paris. So much of the original funds raised went to building the port, there were scant funds for ships and initial cargo for trade.

Despite undercapitalization, trading posts were established in India at Surat in 1668, and Masulipatnam in 1669. Ports were established on islands of

---

[57] Donald C. Wellington, French East India Companies, A Historical Account and Record of Trade, Hamilton Books, Lanham, Md., 2006, at 25.
[58] Madagascar was French until 1975, when French businesses were nationalized, French citizens jailed, and assets frozen. Madagascar was a haven for pirates, domain of Captain Kidd, captured in Madagascar in 1701 and executed. Frederick Quinn, The French Overseas Empire, Praeger, West Port, Conn. 2000, at 152.

Bourbon and Île-de-France, known as Réunion and Mauritius. France never established a Madagascar trade port.

The fortified French port in Pondicherry became the center of its intra-Indian Ocean exchange by 1673. Ships made round trips without incident. Pondicherry remained in French control until 1949, its one enduring bastion in a tumultuous East India history.

The FEIC paid 10% dividend to shareholders in 1675, despite reduction in number of ships in the fleet. The company was burdened by debt owed to the king, largely for attempts to populate Madagascar. In 1682, the king abruptly ended the FEIC monopoly. It was cast into open competition with only five ships in the FEIC fleet.

Colbert died in 1683, leaving directors without a strong leader. Directors hoped imported textiles would garner huge returns, but instead ignited war with domestic producers. The matter settled with an agreement that the company import textiles only for re-export. Directors awarded themselves more dividends.

There was a new generation of directors by 1697. Rather than prioritize commerce, they focused on maximizing earnings through creative financing. Directors obtained a large loan secured on credit of the company, its directors, and shareholders. The immediate effect was a reduction in number of directors and shareholders. New debt was used for interest payments and another dividend, rather than extinguish old debt.

The king renewed the monopoly in 1701. Directors derived income from leasing rights to routes. By 1714, the company had no ships, no cargoes for sale, and no business except leasing privileges garnered from monopoly rights.

## John Law and Financial Restructuring

John Law, a Scottish economist, was another rogue guiding the French East India Company through its roller coaster history. He created such distaste in France for banks that French financial businesses use *credit* rather than the blasphemous *"B"* word.

Law was born into a family of Edinburgh bankers in 1671. He had a brilliant mind for numbers and entered the family business at age fourteen. He preferred using his talents at gaming tables. At seventeen his father died, and he was free to play cards for a living.

Law left England in a hurry after a death sentence in 1694. He killed a man in a duel over a young woman. His sentence was reduced to a fine, but he went into exile avoiding pursuit by the brother of the deceased. Exile took him to Paris and the court of Louis XV.

Extravagances of Louis XIV left a legacy of debt for Louis XV. Law was not concerned about gold-backed currency. His theory was value was in the amount of credit existing for needs of trade, not trade goods. Applying his theory, Law urged the king to establish a state-chartered bank, with power to issue paper currency. With currency Louis XV paid his creditors. Louis XV made Law Controller General of Finances for France.[59]

The first bank chartered by the king was a private bank capitalized by investors, not state owned. Paper currency issued by banks was widely accepted. New currency quickly became central to the French economy. People used currency to pay their taxes.

Meanwhile, Law established the Mississippi Company, with the goal of developing the French colony of Louisiana in North America. In 1716 and 1717 good dividends were paid to shareholders. By 1718, the private bank was converted to a royal bank with unlimited powers to issue bank notes. Bank branches opened in several French cities. Bank loans to shareholders of the Mississippi Company gave the bank company shares as security.

By 1719, Law turned his attention to economics of international trade. The French East India Company needed a financial boost. Directors authorized issuance of fifty thousand shares of stock, some purchased by Law to drive up the price. Further stock subscriptions were only open to original shareholders. The royal bank issued loans for stock purchases.

The king assigned tax income to the FEIC, and the company gave the government funds to pay off debt. To fund the loan to the government, more

---

[59] Law offered his theories to Scotland in 1707, but Scots demurred.

stock was issued. Before the end of the year, Law reorganized the FEIC to include trade in Louisiana, Canada, India, and Far East islands. Stock prices of the FEIC soared 400%.

As Controller General, Law demonetized gold. He planned to do so for silver. He stopped purchases of bank shares, causing the price of shares to fall by 20%. Law refused to peg bank notes at a constant value, or issue more shares. The public revolted and Law was removed as Controller General. Share prices dropped to half of what they were in 1719. In a royal panic, Law was reinstated. He put gold and silver currency back into circulation and began buying notes. By late 1720, paper currency was no longer legal tender. East India Company shares went back to pre-1719 value.

The French stock crash had catastrophic impact across Europe but had delightful effect for the French monarchy. Royal debt was eliminated by public purchases of stock. Worthless stock had no redemption due from the government. The public held the government debt. John Law was public enemy number one. Escaping execution again, Law left on a December evening in 1720, for Brussels. He died in poverty in Venice in 1729.

Law's legacy for the FEIC was not all negative. The company operated thirty ships by the end of 1719. The FEIC built more warehouses and its trade monopoly extended to 1770.

On the downside, FEIC was still saddled with futile desire of the monarch for a settlement in Madagascar. French settlement in Louisiana was also futile. Benefit to FEIC in North America was in its tobacco monopoly.

At this point, FEIC was an odd organization. Its stock was privately owned, but choice of directors and control over operations vested in the king. Everyone profited from tobacco, as the FEIC taxed production and the crown received import duties on crops.

## Dabbling in Indian Politics

A roadblock to development of French trade in India was prior English presence. The English had sixty years of developing local contacts. Frenchman Joseph Francois Dupleix learned from British experiences as he planned for the French to overtake the British.

Dupleix made friends with rulers in the Mogul Empire of southern India. French traded at Pondicherry, in Mogul territory. In 1744, when the French and British went to war, coincidently the Mogul Empire was disintegrating. War ended in a draw.

In 1757, British-backed rulers in India ousted French supported monarchs. At the Battle of Plassy, three thousand English troops defeated an army of fifty thousand. Britain gained dominance in India. France was left with only a trading station at Pondicherry.

Despite ups and downs of the FEIC, Lorient continuously improved operations. By 1723, there were seventy-six company owned ships. Eight ships docked in any given year. More cargo was carried in peacetime when ships did not also carry guns.

By mid-century, there was much criticism in France of the FEIC. Its favored relationship with the crown, allowing government help when management faltered, was the subject of a scathing public report. The Council of State removed FEIC's trade monopoly. The crown took control of company assets. FEIC kept Lorient port, profiting from services.

English distraction with the American Revolution gave France a period of dominance in the Far East. Distraction was short lived. Although the French East India Company had a corporate structure, it was no longer in control of French foreign trade.

## The Second French East India Company 1785-1789

In 1785, FEIC was reborn as the East India and China Company. The king granted a monopoly for all trade past Cape of Good Hope. Ships launched from Lorient to Canton, Pondicherry, the Bengal Coast, Mahé, Mauritius, Madagascar, Maldives, Siam, Indochina, and Japan. King Louis XVI named twelve directors and financed fifteen ships.

Directors received a dividend of 18% in 1788 and 16% in 1789. The new company did not own ports, have diplomatic rights in foreign affairs, and there were no taxes from tobacco. The new company was dependent upon the French navy for protection. From 1786 to 1789, the company returned profits from trade goods. Everything changed in May 1789.

The French Revolution began in May 1789. The company lost its royal-granted monopoly. All imports were taxed. The company stayed in business with reduced sailings.

Jacobins took control in October 1793. They seized company property and put directors in jail. Shareholders lost investments and company officers lost their heads. A few directors evaded the guillotine by hiding in a mental hospital. The government paid creditors.

In 1795, after the Reign of Terror passed, there were three ships and ten surviving shareholders of FEIC. They brought legal action against the government to restore property. Battle in the court lasted to 1875. Shareholders received little for fortunes they held prior to the revolution. One matter was undisputed. It was the end of the FEIC.

French foreign presence waned in the 19th century. In 1803, Napoleon sold the Louisiana Territory to the United States. By 1815, there were only West Indian sugar islands and scattered African and Asian posts in French hands. The last vestige of French holdings in India came in 1949, when the French lost Pondicherry.

## Lorient Sans the French East India Company

At the end of the 18th century, Napoleon gave new life to Lorient as shipyards retooled for warships. It was Napoleon's primary naval yard. During World War II, Germans made Lorient the center of German naval operations in the Atlantic. Residents of Lorient fled during Allied bombing. When smoke cleared, everything was gone.

This story ends in a circle. Lorient began as a FEIC facility to replace Port Louis. Today the museum of the French East India Company is housed, not in remnants of Lorient, or a facility on the western bay, but in Port Louis, at the 16th century Spanish fort.

# CONTRACT - SEVILLE
## Columbus Brings Suit in Contract[60]

*Columbus Residence Gran Canaria*

*Full Size Model of the Niña in Gran Canaria*

*Columbus Residence Genoa*

---

[60] At the time of publication, accepted narrative on Columbus in the United States was derogatory. CTH publications are predicated on presentation of competent evidence, without bias. The reader is the jury.

The Admiral of the Ocean went where no one before he had gone. He was ten years seeking support for his venture, governmental and financial. He was criticized for a wild plan to traverse an ocean, which advisors to two kings and a queen said was too far, too speculative, and too likely to lead to unsafe and unrewarded ends. When he returned from his first voyage, having discovered a new world across the unmapped Atlantic, his contemporaries marginalized his effort as easily done, on the verge of completion by others, and accomplished with the aid of secret maps.

To pacify sponsors, and seek support for more crossings of the Atlantic, Columbus repudiated his finding of a new continent, portraying his discovery as a western sea route to India. To mollify critics, Columbus demurred to a god, whose divine guidance lit his path. Royals of Spain used apologetic ramblings of Columbus in a court action to defeat claims of Columbus and his heirs to contract benefits, by attributing discovery to others.

Columbus was assailed by aspiring rivals as egotistical and a social climber. He was the self-educated son of a weaver, who married above his social station. He was persistent in pursuit of royal financial support for his quest. When he was successful on his first voyage, Columbus was deified by the public and marginalized by competitors. His first biographers were a monk, his son, and a 19th century romantic, who idolized him. Their description of the explorer, who doubled the size of the known world and opened the Atlantic to trade, are the basis of 20th century textbook portrayals of Columbus.

Historians of Christopher Columbus over time traveled through phases of unquestioning adoration, attribution of his accomplishments to others, including Vikings and Amerigo Vespucci, to analyzing his human traits, and attributing all evils of Spain in the New World to Columbus. Vespucci's name adorned the continent, because Amerigo fully appreciated the size of the find, was better connected in the business world, and had more friends in influential places, including the pope. Viewing Columbus in the social context in which he lived may assist those who will judge him in the future.

There are three undisputable facts regarding Columbus: 1. He and all who sailed with him knew the world was round; 2. Queen Isabella did not pawn her jewels to fund the voyage as her jewels were pawned to finance war expelling

Muslims from Spain; and 3. The quest of Columbus to discover new lands began with inspiration in Madeira.

This is the story of Columbus, a talented captain, although a man of little education and low social status, who sought to better his position in society, answer questions that perplexed his father-in-law, and stood against Spanish royals to receive his due in contract for specific performance, by award of hereditary title. His story begins in Genoa, moves to Lisbon, Madeira, Seville, Gran Canaria, and the New World, before ending in Spain. Putting Christopher Columbus into historic context introduces travelers to ports inspiring his life's passion and the man as he was. If he must be judged, fairly judge him.

## Christopher Columbus: Formative Years

Christopher Columbus was born in 1451, into a society of rigid structure and narrow expectations. Unless a man distinguished himself in war or the church, social mobility was against the law. His family were multi-generational weavers in Genoa. They lived in a small, rough stone home outside the city gates.

Christopher's father supplemented family income by operating a tavern. The Columbus family owned property. Though Columbus and his siblings did not go to school, they were sufficiently literate to read the Bible and aid in family business transactions.

At the time Florence was the cultural capital of the Renaissance, Genoa was a center of world trade. In Genoa, medieval traditions melted at the docks. Genoese were merchants not colonizers. Their loyalties ran to families, not to cities, or a royal domain. In the 13$^{th}$ century, Genoese sailors mastered seas of the Mediterranean and Atlantic. By 1465, Chios was a Genoese port for goods distributed throughout the Mediterranean. At age fourteen, Columbus sailed to Chios.

By the early 1480s, Columbus could claim to have sailed, *every sea so far traversed*.⁶¹ In addition to Chios and Eastern Mediterranean, he sailed from England to Ireland and Iceland, along the West coast of Africa, known as the equatorial *gold coast*, that extended to Ghana, and to Atlantic islands of Azores, Madeiras, and Canaries. Part of his on-the-job education included learning to read and speak Spanish and Portuguese. Genoese connections were a birthright. They were connections to a fraternal organization of men not tied to a city. Being Genoese in the 15th century was regarded as an asset by foreign monarchs. Columbus was a man of the world in his mid-twenties. He had Genoese spirit.

When he was twenty-five, Columbus was hired by financier Paolo di Negro as a purchasing agent for Centurione, a Genoese finance and mercantile firm transporting sugar.⁶² It was a life-altering experience. In Funchal, Madeira Columbus befriended another young sugar merchant, Jennin Esmerandt. Residing in the Esmerandt home, Columbus lived like a noble. In 1498, as he prepared for his third voyage across the Atlantic, after achieving nobility by marriage and fame by merit, Columbus was again a guest of the Esmerandts. That home is now part of the city museum of sugar.

Centurione sent Columbus to Madeira to arrange purchase of sugar, with half the funds, ostensibly as a deposit. The balance was due upon receipt of the goods in Genoa. There was a miscommunication, resulting in half the

---

61   Felipe Fernāndez-Armeston, Columbus, Oxford Press, Oxford, 1991, at 19. See also: Zvi Dor-Ner, Columbus & the Age of discovery, Wm Morrow, NYC, 1991; Kirpatrick Sale, The Conquest of Paradise, Knopf, NY, 1991. There are hundreds of Columbus biographies, dozens reviewed for this story until repetition of content was achieved. In the late 1990s, academics pondered whether Columbus loved his mother, had friends, sailed with female sailors, and several symposiums were held on whether Columbus was Portuguese or Spanish, even though he self-identified in a court case as a man of Genoa. Post 21st century academics pondered Columbus politics and his views on slavery, which he detested and for which Spaniards sent him to Spain in chains lest he ruin their plantation system.
62   In the mid-15th century, the Genoese Centurione firm had offices in Crimea, Mallorca, Lisbon, Rouen, Antwerp, Bruges, and Bristol. The firm was hard hit by the Turkish conquest of Constantinople and advocated a new world currency on the gold standard. The firm financed discovery to the New World.

desired sugar sent to Genoa, paid in full. The firm accused Columbus of self-dealing in the remaining half of the sugar shipment. The firm pressed the matter in court in Madeira, where Columbus explained he was not a thief, nor had he instigated an independent sugar deal.[63] Regardless of his deficiency in business communication, there was no missing sugar. The matter resolved, and Columbus left Genoa and his employer. By 1477, Columbus was in Lisbon.

There is a story of Columbus arriving in Lisbon. So often repeated, it may be true and may be an invention of early biographers. In the story Columbus was on a Spanish merchant vessel when attacked by French corsairs. The ship sunk. Columbus grabbed an oar and swam six miles to shore in Lisbon.[64] He was incoherent for days. The story explained how Columbus landed penniless in a new place, having lost memory of his early life.

In Lisbon, Columbus worked for his brother Bartholomew, making maps. To meet young ladies after work, Columbus went to church. There he met Dona Filipa Moniz. She was of a noble family in Madeira, clearly above a common tradesman. Filipa was attracted to the tall, red-haired, blue-eyed, strong, young man, who stood out among shorter, swarthy Portuguese. Columbus was charming. He had recently come from business in Madeira. They had a common bond. Very soon thereafter, they were married.

The family pedigree of Filipa went back to the 1419 conquest of Madeira by Prince Henry the Navigator of Portugal. Henry brought grape vines from Crete and sugar cane from Sicily to Madeira, enabling winemaking. Gil Moniz, Filipa's grandfather, was a companion to the prince. The prince made Moniz governor for life of Porto Santo, Madeira in 1433. Title was bestowed with the right of inheritance, which made the recipient a noble.

Filipa's father, Bartholomew Perestrelo, inherited the title and position. Perestrelo was an avid mariner, who amassed an impressive library of books and maps. He also brought rabbits to Madeira, devastating the prince's gardens.

By the time Columbus met Felipa, her father was dead twenty years. Her family had status, but modest income. In Columbus, Felipa's mother saw an earnest young man, who might emulate exploration ambitions of her

---

[63] Carol Delaney, Columbus and the Quest for Jerusalem, Free Press, NYC, 2011, at 36.
[64] Ernle Bradford, Christopher Columbus, Viking, NY, 1973, at 27.

late husband. She also saw a husband who would not require a dowry. For Columbus marriage was entrance to nobility.

The young couple married in 1478 and lived in the Perestrelo/Moniz home in Madeira. Their son, Diego was born in 1479, the year Filipa died of illness. Columbus remained in Madeira where his mother-in-law poured into him all she knew of her late-husband's exploration aspirations. She left Columbus to absorb the contents of the Perestrelo library, and map collection. To his practiced knowledge of the seas, Columbus added knowledge of the time. He emerged from Madeira a self-educated man, with a passion.

## The Columbus Reading List

Contrary to 19th century mythology, Columbus and his contemporaries knew the world was round. Columbus combined newly gained knowledge with biblical learning in his early life, as he calculated the distance across the ocean. He leaned toward accepting a short distance from Lisbon to India, palatable to sponsors and sailors.

Modern scholars deride Columbus' calculations, resulting in a football shaped earth. Considering that north and south regions of the globe were not mapped in the 15th century, proportions anticipated by Columbus are reasonable, for a smaller earth. Columbus calculated the circumference of the earth at 19,000 miles, smaller than the actual 24,900 miles. Columbus applied a 4,810 feet mile, not the modern 5,280 feet.[65]

Historians discuss whether Columbus falsified his ship's log to deceive sailors into thinking the journey was not imperceptibly long. Put into historic context, Columbus had an idea of the overland distance from Lisbon to India. His calculations reconciled an assumption the sea route doubled that distance. Not knowing the existence or size of the western hemisphere, existence of the Pacific Ocean, or size of the Arctic and Antarctic accounts for smaller calculations of the earth's circumference.

---

[65] William Phillips and Carla Rahn Phillips, The Worlds of Christopher Columbus, Cambridge U. Press, 1992, at 110.

To Columbus the earth was higher at the equator. He traveled below the equator as a young man. Popular wisdom in his time was the further south a mariner traveled, the warmer the climate. Fires of hell burned in the south. Columbus learned this was true to a point. In his fourth journey he proved climate was variable above and below the equator.

In the 1440s Gutenberg created a typeset printing machine making possible duplication of ancient texts. Wisdom of the world held in a few libraries of monks became widely available. In Madeira, Columbus read printed editions of texts in the Perestrelo library. Examining his reading material provides insight to ideas formulated by Columbus.

Columbus read and made notes in margins of texts, some which he took on voyages. The eclectic array of material described the world as it was known, and thought to be, from received stories of travelers and computations by astronomers and philosophers. Maps included fictional islands, regarded as real in the 15th century.

A basic explorers' text was *Geography*, by 2nd century philosopher Ptolemy, who lived in Alexandria, a world center of knowledge. Ptolemy wrote the world was a sphere, with a continuous land mass adjoined by an ocean. He identified a great southern continent. For fifteen hundred years explorers sought an elusive southern continent.

Ptolemy established the size of the Atlantic as half the circumference of the earth. The calculation accounts for smaller earth assumptions of Columbus. Ptolemy was also a cartographer. His maps were set on a grid of longitude and latitude.

The 1st century Roman mariner, Pliny the elder inspired travel to Antipodes Islands in the Atlantic, in his opus work *Natural History*. Pliny argued there were continents north and south of the known world. His book included cures for gallstones and eye complaints.

A 2nd century Greek, Plutarch, wrote of visions and voices in the air in *Lives*. In lonely days at sea, Columbus reached for this book. The more Columbus told people of ethereal voices guiding him on voyages, the harder it was to find sailors for his ships.

Strabo lived in what is now Turkey during the time of Christ. He traveled terrain of Greek and Roman battles. His travels were recorded in *Geography*. Writings of Strabo were attractive to Columbus as they espoused notions of more land, less ocean.

Two new releases obtained by Perestrelo were *Imago Mundi*, by French Cardinal, Pierre d' Ally, written around 1400, and *Historia Rerum Whique Gestarum*, by mid-15th century Pope Pius II. The cardinal offered calculations of a small earth, with a narrow Atlantic Ocean. He established the length of a degree and length of a solar day at solstice used by mariners calculating progress at sea, employed by Columbus. The Cardinal pondered the end of the millennium as an end to the world. The Pope wrote of riches of the Orient a short distance across the Atlantic. As proof of a short sea passage to India, he relayed a story of Indian merchants landing on German shores in the 12th century.

Hot new releases in the time of Columbus were *The Book of the Marvels of the World*, commonly known as *The Book of Marco Polo*, written in 1300 and printed in 1485, and *The Travels of Sir John Mandeville*, widely printed not knowing the knight was as fictional as his travels.[66] The book was written by a monk accumulating travel reports, spiced with imagined exploits. Both books inspired Columbus and his contemporaries to travel.

Columbus sought more information. He wrote to Paolo Toscanelli, who stated China was 5,000 miles west from Lisbon by sea. Toscanelli died in 1482, but not before sending Columbus maps and charts.[67]

Columbus kept detailed logs of his voyages. Even if Columbus understated the distance to not alarm his crew, the logs added to the body of knowledge. In 1500, on his third voyage, when Columbus was sent from Haiti to Spain in chains, discredited to the royals by the Spanish governor so the explorer would not disrupt the slave economy nobles imposed in the New World, he compiled a *Book of Privileges* with his accomplishments in support of the obligation of his sponsors to his family. The *Book* was evidence in court.

---

[66] For more on Sir John Mandeville, see Cruise through History Itinerary III – Ports of the Eastern Mediterranean.
[67] Bradford, at 55.

# Politics, Personality, Persistence and Patronage

In 1453 Constantinople fell to Muslims. The Christian world was cut off from its Eastern capital. Even more critical, Europe was cut off from overland trade routes East. Prince Henry the Navigator mused about a sea-route to India early in the 15th century. By mid-century, a route to India by sailing west into the Atlantic was an imperative.

From the time Columbus was born, discovery of a sea route to India was a hot topic at the ports. Royals offered rewards for discovery. Financiers offered funding for such a voyage.

Only a royal on behalf of a domain could claim new real estate. The pope sanctioned land acquisition and resolved disputes. Royals were responsible for settlers, used their armies for defense, and most important, established authority over profits from trade in new turf. Royals, the discoverer, the royal governor, and financiers divided profits. A commoner like Columbus could live as a royal for life if he discovered new lands.

From the time Columbus formulated his quest, to receipt of a royal contract in 1492, he spent a decade selling his plan. As a man of Genoa, Columbus was agnostic in choice of a royal sponsor. He went first to King João II of Portugal. The king was disposed to support discovery, but not on terms demanded by Columbus for title and compensation. While the king left Columbus waiting for an answer, in 1487 he gave a royal commission to Flemish explorer Ferdinand Von Olmen to test feasibility of the Columbus plan. [68] Von Olmen's ships embarked from the Azores and returned in two months without success.

Meanwhile, Columbus approached the king of England, whose ships attempted sailing west. English captains reported the quest unattainable. King Henry VII sent ships each year from 1491 until 1498, when he finally learned of discovery of Newfoundland and Nova Scotia by father and son John and Sebastian Cabot in 1497.[69]

---

[68] Fernández-Armeston, at. 47.
[69] Bradford, at 72. The Cabots were Venetians, who sailed for England.

Next, Columbus traveled to Spain, where he followed King Ferdinand and Queen Isabella around the country seeking an audience. Even critics of Columbus were awestruck by his persistence. The king and queen were impressed by detailed research and maps presented by Columbus. As much as reaching India intrigued them, they had a higher priority of expelling Muslims from Spain. When Cordova was conquered in 1492, they were ready to talk to Columbus. Columbus had given up on Spanish royals and was headed to France.

## Admiral of the Ocean

Rebuked by Spain, Columbus rode from Cordova on a donkey, headed to La Rábida monastery to collect his young son, Diego. In a climactic moment, Columbus was overtaken by a messenger from the Spanish court and invited to return. Historians disagree whether the king overruled the queen's advisors, or the queen had a personal affinity for Columbus. Regardless, King Ferdinand and Queen Isabella etched themselves into every American history book with their decision to back Columbus in 1492.

On August 2, 1492, three vessels with 88 crew left Spain by way of the Canary Islands. Columbus chose the Canaries taking advantage of favorable westerly winds. Choice of route was one of several decisions by Columbus enabling a successful voyage.

In transit, Columbus realized magnetic north and North Star were variable to the west and east. He completed Toscanelli's charts and deleted mythical islands from maps. Sailors benefited from his notes, even as they marginalized his accomplishments. Had Columbus not altered course southwest to avoid a mutiny, he would have landed on Florida. Years later, one of his sailors, Ponce de Leon, had that honor.

The Bible said parrots were in Eden. Haiti had parrots. Therefore, Haiti was Eden. Columbus wrote glowing reports of the island and natives, before he left 39 sailors on land. Having lost *Santa Maria*, smaller ships could not accommodate a consolidated crew.

On the return, winds deposited Columbus on Portuguese turf in the *Nina*, while owner and captain of the *Pinta* was first to reach Spain. He claimed the discovery. Queen Isabella pouted over the Portuguese landing, but waited for Columbus to return to Spain, where he was a greeted as a national hero.

Spain balked at payments due to Columbus and his heirs, and initially refused inheritable noble title, offers upon which Columbus relied when he took risks crossing an unmapped ocean. Columbus sued in Spanish court for specific performance on a contract.

Spain claimed the Pinta captain was first in discovery of the New World. The court case resolved in 1556, fifty years after the death of Columbus, in favor of the Columbus family.

Queen Isabella, always a staunch supporter of Columbus, died in 1504, just as Columbus returned from his 4$^{th}$ voyage. King Ferdinand was faithful to the Columbus family. He arranged the marriage of Diego to the niece of a duke, reinstated his inheritance as governor of Hispaniola discovered by Columbus, and awarded him a large pension.

Pope Alexander VI resolved disputes to the New World by Catholic countries Spain and Portugal. In 1493, a papal bull granted Spain all lands Columbus discovered and would discover beyond a line drawn north to south 375-400 degrees west of the Azores. This Treaty of Tordesillas gave Brazil, Cape Verde, and the west coast of Africa to Portugal, and the unknown New World to Spain. Columbus was made Admiral of the Ocean.

Spanish monarchs granted Columbus a second voyage, consisting of 17 ships and 1300 men. A big parade celebrated the launch. The winds were favorable. Crossing time short. Columbus landed on Lesser Antilles and discovered Puerto Rico, Guadalupe, and Cuba, which he declared a mainland. Reception in Haiti was not good. There were no survivors.

Columbus was an able promoter and sailor. He was a failure as a civic administrator. He wished to be governor of Haiti, establishing hereditary rights of noble title for his heirs. Columbus preferred discovery of new lands. He left colony management to his brother.

The first colonists were opportunists, not farmers. They enslaved natives. Europeans demanded European conveniences sent from Spain, rather than eat local food. The second voyage was cut short so Columbus could run back to Spain and curtail rebellion. He begged the Queen to send a strong administrator to deal with lazy adventurers.

On the third voyage to the New World, Columbus proved he was a genius at sea and a failure on land. The voyage began well in June 1496, with a stop where his life as an explorer began, in Madeira, at the home of the Esmerandts. The voyage was financed in part by his former employer, the Centurione firm.

For this voyage Columbus chose a southerly route. He believed gold was found in warmer climates and weather was warmer the further south he sailed. Columbus sailed from the Canaries to Cape Verde, then to the mainland of Venezuela. He sailed within sight of the Orinoco River as it poured with great force into the ocean. Recognizing fresh water of such magnitude came from a great landmass, in 1496 Columbus wrote, "I believe this is a very large continent which until now has remained unknown."[70] He was careful to use words of the papal bull. He then sailed to Trinidad across the Gulf of Paria.

In 1498 or early 1499, Columbus sailed to Haiti. He found his brother abandoned the town site of Isabella for Santo Domingo and rebellion was in full force. When a new governor arrived, he put Columbus, his son, and his brother in chains and sent them to Spain. Columbus discovered a New World in 1492 and was banned from Hispaniola in 1500.

The trip to Spain was difficult for Columbus. Storms made sailing unpleasant. He retreated into visions and listened for mystic voices that comforted him on past voyages. He felt victimized by enemies, unappreciated by royals, and guilty for loss of status for his heirs. In 1499, Vasco da Gama reached India by sailing around the Cape of Good Hope. Bartholomew Diaz conquered the Cape in 1488. At the age of 50 Columbus was undone. He offered to lead a campaign to the Holy Land. The proposal was not career enhancing.

Reports to the Queen from Hispaniola improved, as did accumulation of gold. Columbus was authorized to explore again if he did not set foot in Santo

---

[70] Fernández-Armeston, at 128. Columbus left the area by 1498. Amerigo Vespucci arrived not before 1499, with Alonso d' Hojeda, seeking pearls described by Columbus. Vespucci claimed arrival in 1497, on an unknown ship.

Domingo. In 1502, he managed financing for four vessels and a small crew of old men and young boys. The queen offered to release criminals if they would sail with Columbus. Few took the offer.

Gale force winds blew the fourth voyage of Columbus from Gran Canarias to Santo Domingo in twenty-one days. Although Columbus tried warning the governor of the coming storm, he refused Columbus shelter. Instead, the governor launched nineteen ships, holding 500 men and a cargo of gold headed to Spain. All was lost at sea. On board were leaders of rebellion against Columbus. A ship leaving Santo Domingo a few days later arrived safely in Spain. That ship carried the share of gold due to Columbus.

On the fourth voyage, Columbus added Belize, Panama, and Honduras to his New World. In worm-infested ships Columbus was unable to reach Florida. He shipwrecked in Jamaica. Columbus dazzled locals with his ability to predict a total eclipse of the sun.

Columbus returned to Spain late in 1504. Queen Isabella died weeks later. For two years Columbus pursued his contract rights. He died in 1506, which did not end his travels.

Columbus was interred in a Franciscan church in Valladolid in Spain. On his third voyage, Columbus wore robes of a Franciscan. In 1509, his family transferred his remains to Seville, near a home given to Columbus by Isabella. Relics of the Admiral were reinterred in Santo Domingo until conquest by Napoleon in 1795. Columbus bones went to Havana. In 1898, Cuba was liberated from Spain and remains of Columbus returned to Seville.

Today guides at Seville Cathedral believe remains of Columbus are behind his monument. Locals in Santo Domingo are equally adamant the Admiral of the Ocean lies on the island of his first discovery. Scientific testing is inconclusive, so the answer is personal choice.

## He Made It Look So Easy, Anyone Could Have Done It

The Columbus legacy was numerous explorers seeking to outdo him. Search for a western sea route to India continued for 200 years. Dozens of explorers tried and failed.

*Columbus Made Discovery of a New World Look Easy*

There is a story of Columbus at a banquet in Barcelona. Aspiring explorers belittled Columbus for his reception as a hero. In response, Columbus put an egg on the table and invited anyone to sit the egg upright. Several men tried and none succeeded. Columbus tapped the egg lightly, crushing the bottom, and set it upright. He said, "it always looks easy when you know how to do it." If the story is not true, it is still a fitting allegory.

The 19th century writers Ralph Waldo Emerson and Washington Irving complained America was named for a thief.[71] Amerigo Vespucci was Florentine, working for powerful Medici. Today, Columbus critics offer contemporary narratives as evidence, judging the past. Judge the past as one will, facts are facts.

---

[71] Delaney, at 233

# ZONING – SPAIN & SPANISH NEW WORLD

## Law of the Indies

*Colima Town Square*

*Chiapas Town Square*

*Leon Nicaragua City Grid*

*Los Angeles El Pueblo*

In 1492, Columbus opened a new world of possibilities for Spain. Other explorers increased turf, under Vatican-granted authority to render the New World Catholic. Spain and Portugal were initial contenders for new territory. In 1580 Philip II of Spain received control of Portugal. Portugal gave Spain far-flung territory, extending to the Philippines. Philip also inherited the Spanish Lowlands of Netherlands and Belgium, Corsica, and Two Sicilies, comprising southern Italy and Sicily.[72] Philip was a narrow-minded monarch, who desired his vast domain be Catholic and organized under strict rules of conformance.

Centuries before Britain's colonies ringed the globe, upon which the sun never set, Spain held areas of California to Florida, Central and South America, populated by indigenous people the Spanish called Indians. Spain enabled Franciscan friars in the New World to enslave Indians in the name of religious salvation. Friars established missions, Spanish soldiers lived in presidios, and wealth-seeking civilians began pueblos.[73]

A desire for conformance in control led to Law of the Indies. Spain decreed slave status of Indians and structure for its satellite domain. By 1680, Law of the Indies dictated town planning for the New World from the western hemisphere to the Philippines. The effect of Spanish zoning rules can be seen at the historic core of Los Angeles California, despite its sprawl, and towns begun as Spanish pueblos, from hill towns of Mexico to Nicaragua.

Spanish zoning rules were simple and absolute. Stamp of the Law of the Indies is evident today, though colonies gained independence a century ago. Philip the tyrant left an attractive legacy travelers enjoy. This story is a guide to zoning in the Law of the Indies.

---

[72] Philip married Queen Anne of England, daughter of Henry VIII and his Spanish first wife. Parliament kept Philip contained as a consort, never king. Philip and Anne made the state religion Catholic. He proposed to Elizabeth I. His disdain for her return of England to Protestant, ruled by a mere girl, led to the Spanish Armada and another story.

[73] See Cruise through History – Itinerary 7 – Ports of the Pacific Coast of North America – California.

# Spanish Zoning Law

Zoning organizes communities, making evident community priorities. In the European medieval world, towns began as market centers. People crammed into housing on streets meandering organically as streams from a source. Often towns remained close to sources of water for mills, human needs, and transportation. Markets were the priority.

In the world of Philip II, the Catholic church was the central priority. Law of the Indies required new towns organized on a central square, the Plaza Mayor. At the top of the square, most prominent was the church. Town halls and government buildings, less prominent than the church, were to sides and across the square were market shops. Emanating from the central square, a grid of neat, straight streets were places for homes. Farms were close to town, yet far enough to keep cattle from streets.

Application for founding a town required twelve committed Spanish landowners. Their site selection needed to evidence ability to build a healthy, safe, and viable settlement. Towns required access to dependable sources of water, be defensible from pirates, and have contiguous farmland, able to support the population.

The law was as practical as it was dictatorial. Marshes were known unhealthy even when vectors of disease were unknown. Ponce de Leon began his town in swamp land, until settlers appealed to the king to move to healthier ground, they called Puerto Rico. Havana began set back from the opening to the harbor, thought defensible from pirates. Pueblo Los Angeles in Alta California territory was in proximity to vast farmland. The law authorized a hospital next to the church. Contagious patients were housed out of town.

In each instance of Alta California settlements there were indigenous people enslaved as farmers and laborers building the town. Proximity to slaves was a dictate of the Law. Established communities of native people, with farms and water sources, were co-opted as foundations of Spanish towns. Today there exists no tribal land in Los Angeles County.

Aesthetics were important in Spanish law. Towns were required to have a uniform style. Spain's authorized towns in the New World were distinctive for tile roofs, tile floors, stucco walls, and arched porticos. Where timber was plentiful, ceilings had exposed beams and heavy wooden doors. In affluent market towns, buildings were embellished with carvings, heavy window lintels, and elaborate moldings, known as Spanish baroque.

On the edge of each town is a cemetery. In Spanish tradition, cemeteries are elaborate. People impoverished in life were made elegant in death. Heaven was paradise. Wealthy of the town had family crypts as in Spain. Modest folk built simple structures, painted in bright colors. On Sundays and Catholic feast days, the family meal could be enjoyed in the cemetery, with spirits of ancestors.

Law of the Indies required slaughterhouses, fisheries, and tanneries away from town. Residents were spared smells and unsightly refuse. Rancheros kept cattle out of town.

# Historic Pueblos Preserved

LOS ANGELES - Missions did not endure in Los Angeles. In 1785, a twenty-five-year-old Gabrieleño woman, Toypurina, led her people in revolt of onerous conditions under which her people labored in Mission San Gabriel.[74] The mission was aptly named for lands of Gabrieleño people, taken by Spanish, upon which missions were built. To resolve the uprising, people were given liberty to stay at the mission or move to ranchos, lands of civilian owners, on which they worked. Today there are no Indian Reservation lands in Los Angeles or Orange County. Toypurina died in 1799, in Mission San Juan Bautista.

From mission lands, after secularization of missions in 1833, 33,000 acres was granted for Los Angeles. In 1835, it was designated capital of Alta California, of Mexico. By the time Alta California was part of the United States, in the 1848 Treaty of Guadalupe Hidalgo, a large agricultural area between the pueblo and Los Angeles River was planted in vines imported from Bordeaux. Los Angeles shipped wine to San Francisco.

---

[74] Gabrieleño is the Spanish name for people, who refer to themselves as Tongva, non-federally recognized.

After World War II, Los Angeles was a beneficiary of the post-war economic boom. The population grew quickly, as educational institutions and employers located in the city of sunshine and opportunity. Diverse interests and growing philanthropy of civic leaders resulted in a plethora of museums, in the core city. The tiny pueblo Plaza Mayor is preserved, marking founding of the city. It is ringed by mid-18th century hotels.

Colima – Comala – Chiapas - Throughout the 17th and 18th centuries, Spain built a string of colonial hill towns, along the Pacific coast, for the purpose of mining gold, silver, and lead. Rarely were dreams of riches in New Spain realized. At most, little hill towns of Spanish Colonial Mexico were farm and government administration centers.

Colonial hill towns of Colima, Comala, and Chiapas were plotted in classic Spanish city planning, with a cathedral on the central town square. Buildings around the square, and radiating out into a grid of streets, were low and simple, stucco homes and businesses. In the modern era, people left towns for opportunities in large cities. Remnants of colonial history sit preserved. Today, they are gems for travelers looking for the real old Mexico.

Colonial towns were set back in the hills, as a defense against pirates, who trolled coasts. Still, it was necessary to receive goods at a port. Over time, port villages overcame hill towns in size and importance, such as Puerto Vallarta, with old roads linking to Manzanillo. Manzanillo thrived as a fishing port in the Spanish era, with its protected harbor. Today Manzanillo enjoys rejuvenation as a capital of sport fishing.

Colima was founded in 1523, by Spanish emissaries of the king, who designated it capital of the region, served by port Manzanillo. Iconic of Spanish hill towns, arranged on a grid, emanating from the main square, on which the focal point is a cathedral, Colima was intended to be grand. The Cathedral of Colima is a minor basilica, built in 1894, to overwhelm the square as a beacon to farmers, who looked up to the double bell tower, visible down a long street. The high alter is capped by a grand dome.

The building growing from the side of the basilica is the two-story state government palace. No longer serving that purpose, the space and neoclassical grandour of the building was an assumption by city fathers that the city was destined to greatness. The clock installed in the tower was imported from Germany. The bell tower adds to the appearance of government as part of the church.

The town square of Colima is a densely landscaped park, of lush shade trees and inviting benches. Remaining three sides of the square have buildings with deep, arched portico, where shoppers stroll after church, out of the sun. One side is a hotel and café today, one side is occupied by shops, and the remaining side holds the regional history museum.

Dedication of the park to Miguel Hidalgo, the father of Mexican liberation from Spain, is more than a tribute. Colima was Hidalgo's parish in 1792, where he entertained future leaders of the revoltuion. Hidalgo's famous march from Delores Hidalgo to Guanajuato ignited revolvtion decades later. Colima was central to liberation of coastal Mexico.

Over a century ago, Colima was appreciated as a showpiece. Today, tourism gives reason for the city to maintain the square and several streets deep in shops and functioning government offices. Colima has international recognition for maintaining historic beauty and 21st century relevance as a still-thriving city.

Comala was always the modest sister to Colima. Its streets are lined with single level, white-washed adobe buildings. Comala church, with two short towers and small dome, dominates the small Plaza Mayor. Buildings surrounding the plaza have arched portico, simply less deep than Colima and sans ornamentation.

When the Spanish arrived, indigenous Nauhtl people were enslaved in encomiendas. The system of land grants to military leaders were expected to derive income, using local labor. Indigenous farmers rented little plots, formerly held as communal lands.

When in Comala, sit on a bench in the plaza with locals and have a bottle of ponche. The local drink is unique and not quite a beer. So it is in Comala, the little hill town, that is more Nahuatl than Spanish, despite adherence to the Law of the Indies.

Chiapas sits at an awkward cross-section of politics and cultures, as a perennial place of upheaval. The farthest Mexican state from the US border, it is among the most poor. Puerto Chiapas, the port town, on the Pacific coast, is near the border with Guatemala. People are descendent of pre-Maya and pre-Aztec ancient cultures of the region.

Chiapas grew organically, rather than as a planned Spanish city. The church sits on a side street, one street back from the plaza mayor. The plaza has a bandstand in the center, oriented as a marketplace for farmers, not a government center.

Streets of Chiapas are lined with adobe, single level, connected houses and shops. Absent are large hacindas and regal buildings of a Spanish city. Walls are painted bright colors, more indicative of Maya villages of Guatemala, than colonial hill towns of Mexico.

LEON NICARAGUA is a classic Law of the Indies city. Spaniard Gil Gonzáles Dávila landed in Nicaragua 1519. He named the land Nicaragua, for lovely lakes. Finding natives with gold, the conquistador confiscated all he could and fled to Panama.

Once in Panama, the founder of Panama City, Pedrarias Dávila, relived Gil of his gold. Pedrarias the Cruel led Balboa to an early grave. Gold made Nicaragua attractive.

Among gold-seeking Spanish was Francisco Hernandez de Córdoba. He founded Leon on the Pacific Coast. Today currency of Nicaragua is known as Cordoba in his honor.

Arriving conquistadors vanquished locals, then fought among themselves. Pedrarias relieved Córdoba of his gold and territory. By 1570, Leon was the capital of New Spain.

Through the 17th and 18th centuries Spanish slave economies flourished in Nicaragua. In 1610, Leon was devastated by volcanic eruption. Pirates on the lake came next.

Welshman Henry Morgan, scourge of Panama, came up the San Juan River in canoes in 1665. Along the Mosquito coast, Morgan added Miskito sailors to his unsavory cadre. Morgan respected Miskito men for vigor and strength under adverse experiences.

Another English pirate, William Dampier, arrived on the Pacific coast of Nicaragua in 1655. His targets were Leon and Granada. Dampier left maps and diaries of his exploits. Ships of the British royal navy came to the Mosquito Coast a century later in 1762. The British enlisted or conscripted Miskito sailors.

The man who tested Spanish control on the San Juan River was young Horatio Nelson. At age twenty-three and an experienced captain, Nelson displayed bravery in his first command of soldiers in a land-assault. The British objective in 1780 was capture of Leon, enabling British cross-oceanic control of commerce. Nelson failed to take the fortress guarding Leon but succeeded in his ascent to British national hero.

Today Leon displays the height of zoning in the Law of the Indies. The elegant cathedral dominates Plaza Mayor, while flanking government buildings await restoration. Straight streets emanate from the square, with single story attached homes and shops. On these streets lived several poets of Leon, memorialized in Poets Corner of the cathedral. Poets of Leon were national ambassadors, church leaders, and a presidential assassin. They were not lawyers. Their stories are held for another volume.

Once recognized as the organization of a town, where the church dominates, Law of the Indies examples span the former Spanish world. Philip was a harsh fellow, who left a legacy of lovely landscapes.

# BANKING -GENOA
## Financing Columbus & Marco Polo

*Genoa Centurione Bank*

Two train stops from popular Ligurian coast cities of Portofino and San Margarita is the historic power-port city of Genoa. Often by-passed by tourists, Genoans conduct business as they have for 800 years. This was home to 15th century power brokers. Their massive homes sit along Garibaldi Street, now home to modern banks, offering cash machines.

Between powerful families of Genoa there were few alliances. Shakespearean lore of Romeo and Juliette was based on Ghibellines, those who supported royalist stand-ins for kings of Spain or France, and Guelfs, those who defended popes and supported republic city councils. In Genoa, the Ghibelline Doria family, and their supporters the Spinola family, faced off against the Fieschi family and supporters the Grimaldis. By the end of this story, all were weakened or left town, leaving rising families of power, such as Centurione to step forward and prosper.

Most prominent on the Genoa harbor is the fancifully painted Centurion Bank, continuously doing business since its directors hired young Christopher Columbus as a sugar merchant and funded travels of the Polo family. Deep in the bank, original rooms have drop slots for harbor payments. Behind steel and glass doors business continues.

This is a brief story of a city of commerce of such wealth that it required a bank and of the bank that funded explorers and kings. The gold standard and double column accounting began in this inauspicious place. Low key and private was how business was done, so as not to attract pirates and competitors.

## Genoa Banking Capital of Medieval Europe

Narrow, winding, dark streets of old Genoa open to small plazas with grand churches. Notable of older churches is San Lorenzo, with a crypt to rival the Vatican. As the city expanded from the harbor it moved up the steep hill to the castle/fortress. Today an elevator takes visitors to the vista terrace for a spectacular view of the city and harbor.

The old harbor is in active use as it has been for 800 years. Centuries ago, a raised and arched pedestrian promenade ringed the harbor. Today a raised freeway takes its place. A modern aquarium sits on the harbor, surrounded by small craft and a new NH hotel.

Genoa has a home-born saint, Saint Virginia Centurione Bracelli, the daughter of Giorgio Centurione, a bank founder, was born in 1587. She is the patron saint of Mount Calvary convent in hills above Genoa. She married at age fifteen, nursed her husband through his mortal illness, then dedicated her considerable fortune to the refuge for the needy she founded, now a convent. She died in 1651 and was canonized in 2003.

Genoa entered prominence in the first wave of the Renaissance, about 1100, when city states of future Italy controlled the Mediterranean. Of power cities Venice, Pisa, Amalfi, and Genoa, Genoa was most powerful. The cities grew as crusader ports sending knights to Jerusalem in the early 13th century. One of the centurions in battles of the crusades, known only as Centurione, was so distinguished, that he returned to Genoa as patriarch of a family of bankers, which became Centurion bank, the bankers funding expeditions of Marco Polo and Columbus, as well as European kings and Tsar Ivan IV of Russia.

Centurione was a newcomer to the power elite of Genoa, which included families of Doria, Fieschi, Spinola, and Grimaldi. Doria and Spinola were Ghibelline. Fieschi and Grimaldi were Guelfs. When Doria and Fieschi went to war in Genoa, the Grimaldis, sympathetic to Fieschi, were less inclined to mount a battle. The Grimaldis went down the coast to Monaco, where they established a family fortress, defended against Doria. Guelfs were banned from Genoa in 1271. When Guelfs returned to power in Genoa by 1297, the Spinola family was banned from Genoa. The Grimaldis liked life better in Monaco. Since 1297 to today, the royal family of Monaco have always been Grimaldi.

Spinola family tyrants ruled Genoa from 1198 to 1297. In a battle between Spinola and Fieschi, Spinola estates were burned. Fieschi transitioned Genoa to a ruling council of sixteen citizens. Spinola fought back, aided by Doria.

Doria knights were leaders of troops in the crusades. Many years later a Doria knight sided with the pope and led troops against Joan of Arc. The family held fiefdoms in Portofino and Sardinia, ruled from the family seat in Genoa. Andrea Doria, born in 1451 and living to 1560, (yes 109 years), became wealthy as a captain with an independent navy for hire. Prior to unification of Italy in 1862, southern Italy and Sicily were controlled by kings of Spain or France. In 1528, Doria sent his navy on behalf of France to oust Spain. He then fought with Spain to oust France when the king of France defaulted on his fee.

The Fieschi family were staunch supporters of popes and favored democratic representation in governing councils, rather than autocratic power of Doria lords. The Fieschi dynasty included Pope Innocent IV and Adrian V, in addition to 72 cardinals and 300 bishops and archbishops. They held land in central and southern Italy and Sicily. When the Holy Roman Emperor Frederick II imprisoned Pope Innocent in 1244, Genoa sent an army to rescue the pope.

In a battle for power in 1547, between Doria and Fieschi, Doria at age 91, battle experienced, with a large, loyal army, defeated 22-year-old Gian Luigi Fieschi. Since the victor writes history, the battle is known as the Fieschi Conspiracy. Gian's dispute was with Andrea's nephew and heir Gianettino. Andrea's dispute was with the pope.

Gianettino was a despicable fellow, womanizer, and drunkard, who was always jealous of the handsome, elegant Gian. Gian was in love with the daughter of Adamo Centurione. Andrea forced Adamo into giving his daughter in marriage to Gianettino. Not satisfied, Gianettino made amorous advances on the eventual wife of Fieschi, a Medici.

In the prelude to battle, Andrea Doria took galley's belonging to the pope from Civitavecchia and held them for ransom in Genoa. The pope conceded land to Andrea for the release of the papal navy. Then the pope summoned Gian to Rome and gave him orders to destroy Andrea. On the night of January 2, 1547, Gian and his friends entered Genoa with daggers under their cloaks, ready to do the pope's bidding.

Gianettino suspected foul play and headed to the Doria armory. He was spotted and stabbed to death by a gang of Guelfs. Decked out in his best suit of armor, Gian went to the Genoa harbor, where he released African slaves from chains on Doria galleys, the rowed vessels of warfare. In leaving a galley, Gian fell off a plank, into shallow water. In the melee around him, no one noticed that young Fieschi lay barely covered in water, unable to lift himself in his heavy suit.

The battle ended with Andrea Doria ordering an army level every Fieschi villa in Genoa and the family fiefdom in Chiavari. Doria's desire was ending the Fieschi bloodline, in retribution for loss of his heir. A young Fieschi at school in Pisa was kept hidden by the family. In Chiavari today the Fieschi family chapel remains, without the Fieschi banner.[75]

Doria retired to his villa in Portofino. The watch tower in the tiny town bears the Doria crest. Tenacious Doria outlived his enemies, peers, and immediate family. When he died, his grandchildren entombed the patriarch in the family crypt in Genoa, fit for a king.

Today quiet Genoa boasts 1500 restaurants, competing with inventive dishes and fresh ingredients, at modest prices. Wander through narrow streets near the harbor to *Soul Kitchen*, or elegant *Damare Restaurantbar*, with cracked mirror décor, for lovely meals.

The city does not attract crowds. Genoa is preserved as an open-air museum of medieval commerce, with continual life. Columbus would find his way around today. Only motorcycles parked in alleyways give a hint that life moved forward in time.

## Centurion Bank of St. George

The success of $12^{th}$ century Genoa, at the core of the old city, is visible today. Domination of commerce across the Mediterranean, centered in Genoa, was led by a core of business consortiums more interested in controlling commodities markets than kingdoms. They focused upon sugar and grain not armies. The $12^{th}$ century Centurion bank founded by the Centurione dynasty of financiers kept books for the pope, local churches, and power broker families of Genoa.

In 1407 the Bank of St. George (Giorgio), as successor to Centurion Bank, was a sovereign wealth fund manager with branches in London, Brussels, and St. Petersburg, transacting business from Gibraltar to Goa. The bank was dominant in sugar markets of Madeira, with warehouses in Chios serving the Mediterranean. Find the crest of the Bank of St. George, a maiden and dragon, in ports of medieval trade.

---

[75] The last Count Lavagne of Chiavari, Adriano Fieschi died in 1858. The Garibaldi family lived in Chiavari from 1060, moving to Nice in 1797. Giuseppe was born in 1807 in Nice, when Nice was part of Italy, and another story.

Directors of the Bank hired young Christopher Columbus as a sugar merchant on assignment in Madeira. The Columbus family home is in Genoa, just outside the city gates. The Bank financed the 3rd voyage of Columbus and travels of Marco Polo. When Genoa expended funds on wars with Venice, the Bank operated vast business operations on behalf of its chief debtor. England, France, and the Dutch chartered East India Companies in the 17th century, while the Bank of St. George competed in trade on behalf of Genoa.[76] The Bank of St. George was closed by Napoleon in 1805, and a new bank, begun in 1987, preserved the historic building in the prominent position on the harbor.

*Dragon & Mermaid Lubeck*

The early Genoa bank is credited with devising a gold standard, to normalize the cost of goods in international trading. During World War I, nations printed money to fund the war, effectively eliminating paper backed in gold. After the war, inflation was rampant. In 1922, world financial leaders met in Genoa, once again normalizing value of currency.

Directors of the Bank of St. George were key families of Genoa. They built grand homes along the only wide straight street in the old city. Today the avenue Via Garibaldi is a World Heritage Site. Modern bank offices occupy former estate homes of bankers.

---

[76] The Fugger German bankers were bankrupted by loans made to Philip II of Spain financing the Spanish Armada in 1588, opening more opportunity for Genoa bankers filling the void in sovereign lending.

# PROBATE/CUSTODY -
## HERCULANEUM
JUSTICE FOR JUSTA

*Herculaneum Justa*

On the afternoon of August 24, 79 CE, the sky turned prematurely dark. With a velocity that precluded any hope of escape, a river of mud swept through the coastal resort town of Herculaneum. Townspeople were swept into the sea or buried by a wave of mud.

At first signs of sparks rising from nearby Mount Vesuvius, some cautious residents of this Roman suburb of Naples left the city. Others boarded ships in the harbor. Captains of ships delaying departure, did so at their peril. Failure to heed warning sparks proved fatal.

While ash covered Pompeii, Herculaneum drowned in volcanic mud. So complete was the coverage, that Herculaneum was forgotten for the next 1600 years. As if guarding the secret city, Mount Vesuvius erupted again in 1631, just as discovery was imminent.

Herculaneum lay hidden, while a new population of beach-loving residents moved into the area, oblivious to what lay beneath their homes. A new road ran from foothills of Vesuvius, to buried gates of Herculaneum, and along the ocean. This was prime real estate, prized for vacation homes of the well to do in the 1st century, so it was in the 18th century. This was the location of a royal palace, the model for the Getty Mansion in Los Angeles, and lavish homes and gardens of wealthy families and bishops.

Over time villas evolved into multi-family housing. Some were hotels. One of the 18th century villas now a hotel is the Villa Miglio d'Oro. The owner retained 18th century charm in the hotel and 1st century features in the garden. From suite windows guests have a view of excavated portions of ancient Herculaneum and the ocean beyond.

This is a story of city life in Herculaneum. The setting spanning two millennia, can be traversed in a few yards. So often museums inhabit former royal palaces. Herculaneum offers a glimpse into life of working people, straining for justice in Roman courts of the day. This case is the story of a young girl, seeking to maintain free status in probate court.

## Herculaneum - Until August 23, 79 CE

Herculaneum was settled by Greeks in the 8th century BCE. To the north, Naples was a major port city. Herculaneum remained a retreat for wealthy merchants. Herculaneum harbor accommodated pleasure craft. Its streets were lined with lavish villas.

Herculaneum existed for its beachside location. The economy was based on pleasure. The city held a theater and baths of a Roman city. There were craft shops, artisans, and wine bars. There were no brothels and no temples in Herculaneum. Pleasure was pervasive leaving no need for contained structures of fun or penance.

Herculaneum was aligned with Pompeii, another city of leisure. In Herculaneum were second homes of an ecumenical mix of Oscan, Samite, and Greek people. The familiar language was Oscan, similar to Latin. Graffiti in ancient Herculaneum evidences a mix of pagans and Jews, named Florus, Manius, and David. Herculaneum estates had slaves.

The best streets faced the ocean and received sea breezes. Ocean view homes were elegant, with lovely courtyards, fountains, and pools. Homes had statues, of which only bases remain. Bodies of a marble population washed out to sea in a river of volcanic mud.

Homes were decorated with mosaics, carvings, and sculptures. Furnishings included sculpted wood tables, of the type reproduced in 18th century Early American and French Provincial furniture. The popular American four poster bed, with posts topped with a pinecone, is copied from Greco-Roman furniture excavated at Herculaneum. Pinecones were a Greek fertility symbol, redefined in 18th century America as symbols of hospitality.

In 61 CE, Apostle Paul came ashore. Evidence of his preaching is seen in a shrine with a simple crucifix in a small, upper floor room of a home. Early Christians prayed covertly.

Vesuvius slumbered, only occasionally throwing forth embers. In 62 CE, the volcano rumbled causing earthquakes. Herculaneum was severely damaged. Wealthy residents of Herculaneum with other options moved from the quake zone, abandoning second homes. Damaged homes fell into disrepair. The population declined. Fine craftspeople servicing a wealthy cliental moved near their patrons.

Herculaneum remained a popular seaside residential area, available to people of lesser means. Residents remodeled former grand villas into shops and multi-family living quarters. The city became a Roman protectorate.

# A Probate/Custody Action – No Justice for Justa

In records of life in Herculaneum, a court case involving child custody survived. The child's name was Justa. Her father was a man of property, and her mother was his slave at the time of Justa's birth. Their dispute puts a a window into 1st century Herculaneum.

After the earthquake of 62 CE impacted Herculaneum, the opportunistic merchant Gaius Petronius seized on vacated real estate to better his accommodations. He moved into a nice house with his wife, a former slave, Calatorius. The couple was unable to have children. Gaius turned to his slave, Vitalis, who gave birth to a girl they named Justa.

Over time Vitalis bought her freedom from Petronius. The three adults remained in the home as parents to Justa. Life at home was amiable until Calatorius gave birth to a child. Calatorius wanted Vitalis out of the household as much as Vitalis wanted a home of her own. Petronius did not want Justa to leave. Vitalis left the home without Justa.

As a freedwoman, Vitalis brought legal action for custody of Justa, who was property of Petronius, as she was born a slave to a slave. In an out of court settlement, Vitalis paid Petronius for his costs of care for Justa. Justa went to live with her mother. Mother and daughter lived a happy and prosperous life. They operated a business together.

Happiness was cut short for Justa. When she was in her early teens, her mother died. Petronius died shortly after Vitalis. Justa continued in her mother's business.

Calatorius never showed maternal concern for Justa. She was attracted to Justa's business assets. Calatorius brought a court action to take Justa as property of the Petronius household and assume control of Justa's assets. Her theory was Justa was a slave, living with her mother while a child, and was property of Calatorius, heir to Petronius' estate.

Justa fought back, claiming she was a freedwoman prior to the death of her mother. Paperwork dispositive of the matter could not be found. When the case came to court a surprise witness came forward. He claimed to be the negotiator in resolution of the custody battle in which Vitalis paid Petronius for Justa.[77]

A judge in Rome heard the case. He took the matter under advisement in 75 CE. The case was still pending decision in 79 CE, when all parties to the case were swept away in mud.

## Herculaneum - August 24, 79 CE

August 24, 79 CE began as any glorious summer day at the beach. Then the earth shook the entire Vesuvius plain from the mountain to Herculaneum. Shaking was felt in Naples. Horrors of the day were recorded by a ship's commander for Emperor Titus, Pliny, and by his nephew, Gaius Plinius Caecilius Secundus, better known as Pliny the Younger.

The elder Pliny left Naples harbor sailing for Herculaneum on a rescue mission. Sensing importance of the event, Pliny wrote throughout the day. At Herculaneum, rocks were strewn on the beach, but he felt no sense of imminent danger. He enjoyed a late lunch and then took a nap. His plan was to sail when the wind shifted.

As Pliny slept, the ship and beach filled with ash. The sky turned dark. A rain of pumice stones awaked Pliny. The sea was then too rough to sail. As Pliny pondered his next move, Sulphur gas permeated his lungs. He, his crew, and intended passengers died.

Meanwhile, in Naples, Pliny the Younger and his mother began an escape. They started in a cart, but the ground was shaking so violently the cart was useless. A cloud of ash descended upon them from the sea. They ran away from the sea into a field of tall grass. The world was in total darkness, except when falling ash ignited grass as they ran.

---

[77] Some researchers assert the witness was Justa's biological father, living in the household. Joseph Jay Deiss, Herculaneum, Thomas Y. Crowell Co., New York, 1966, at 79.

Just when Pliny the Younger felt the world as he knew it ended, daylight appeared. Shapes of other survivors appeared, ash-covered amid grass. By August 26, inhabitants of Naples returned home. Pliny the Younger learned the intact body of his uncle was recovered. It was as though the elder man was merely asleep next to his notes.

Naples remained intact, while Pompeii was covered in hot, molten stone, and Herculaneum was covered in mud. Under weight of mud, mosaics in homes buckled like paper. Across the city, mud was 65 to 85 feet deep. Mud hardened for the next 1,630 years.

## Reclaiming Herculaneum

From 80 to 1630 CE, Herculaneum lay hidden. In 1631, Vesuvius erupted with the same might, sending more rivers of mud, and increasing depth of the buried city. Then in 1709, a monk found slabs of marble impeding his ability to dig a well. Unknown to the monk, he struck upper seats of the theater in Herculaneum. He sold the marble to an Austrian prince building a villa. It never occurred to the monk, or prince, that perfectly cut marble is not natural, regardless of divinity of the finder. The city remained hidden.

Fifty years later, after Spanish forces drove Austrians from Naples, a general directed troops to dig at the site of the monk's well. They worked with haste, not keeping records. They were hunting for treasure. They found little but created a mess.

Pompeii was discovered in 1763. The find changed inquiry in the area. Swiss archaeologist, Karl Webber, impressed authorities with the importance of excavating at Herculaneum.

For the next hundred years, Herculaneum was a world famous phenomenon. Thomas Jefferson included Herculaneum and Pompeii on his world tour. French King Francis I kept excavations going at Herculaneum, when in 1828, France replaced Spain in control. Work came to a halt in 1875, when slumlords objected to tunnels undermining tenement housing developed in streets above Herculaneum in the once lovely neighborhood.

The Italian government took control of excavations at Herculaneum in 1927. Instead of objects sold as decorative ornaments, Italy curated finds in museums, later open to the public. Excavation continues at Herculaneum. Fate of Justa remains under advisement.

*Twelve Tables Erected in Roman Forum*

# CIVIL CODE – ROME
## Twelve Tables to Corpus Juris Civilus

A book of laws in history must include the Twelve Tables of Roman Law. Significance of the law transcends content. The Twelve Tables made open, public, and written, cast in stone, the rights of common men and women. No longer were rights arbitrary and subject to interpretation by lords or disregarded by priests. Common Law, the rules commonly understood in society, were insufficient to protect marginalized people in a culturally diverse population. Express rights moved Romans from Common Law to Civil Law. The Roman Republic began with the Twelve Tables in 449 BCE.

From first posting of the Tables in the Forum in Rome, amendments were proposed. Intended to establish rights of justice, equality, and responsibility, that is punishment, nothing was taken as granted. As universal as death and taxes were desires for explanation, illumination of meaning, and inclusion of nuances in law. The Twelve Tables gave meaning to jurisprudence and job security to judges, lawyers, and stone cutters.

A millennium later the emperor Justinian, sitting safely away from the Roman Senate in Constantinople, issued a restatement of Civil Law in Corpus Juris Civilus. His dynasty engendered riots, resulting in burning the first Hagia Sophia. That is the next story.

The Twelve Tables resounded as the basis for law in republics for over two millennia. James Madison cribbed from the Tables when he drafted the Bill of Rights to the US Constitution. Fortunately, Madison used measured discretion, accepting portions of Roman law which guaranteed fundamental due process, right to trial, and land rights, and jettisoning rules antiquated by the early nineteenth century.

## Twelve Tables of Roman Law

The first two tables provided means for access to court. Civil court in Rome, as it is today, had a plaintiff and respondent. If the respondent, or representative, failed to appear by noon on the day of trial, default judgement was awarded to the plaintiff. Evidence of debt arose from business transactions. There were damages for torts but no punitive damages. Trials always recessed at sunset when wine bars opened.

Table Three directed debts imposed by the court were payable within thirty days. If not paid, the creditor had the option to physically bind the debtor and bring them before the court three times over sixty days. The debtor was thus held in bond. Holding a debtor in bond placed an obligation on the creditor to feed the debtor daily. Feeding a debtor with a large appetite might outweigh the debt.

Rights and limitations of authority of family patriarchs were expressed on Table Four. Men held wives as property. They were allowed no fault dissolution of marriage, by advising their wife to mind her own affairs. Children were also chattel to a head of household. Children could be sold or rented to others to work. If a father offered a son for sale often, the son was a free man. First sons inherited the family estate. A father was obligated to euthanize children born with deformity or deemed unable to function.

In Tables Five and Six women were either daughters, wives, or slaves. Women of any age were regarded as unable to manage their own affairs, requiring their father, husband, or son, in the case of a son as head of household inherited from his father, to act as guardian. Women within a household were chattel, as were household goods. Table Six presumed marriage when a man and woman lived together for one year, if they were of the same social class.

Land law was set forth in Table Seven. Romans were great roadbuilders. Those living near the road were obligated to pay for the road, which assumed the road provided a benefit. If locals refused to keep a road in good repair, travelers were in their rights to trod across the landscape, through a farm.

There are several stories of ways to avoid road tax. One story arose when the great Via Appia was extended from Rome to Brindisi. People in a settlement, hardly a town, in the path of the road, acted as though they were of unsound mind. The folks told Roman soldiers sent to collect taxes that the moon was made of cheese, and they could harvest the image of the moon in a lake with their rakes. Since mental illness spread in the air, soldiers rerouted the road.

Table Seven established rules for settlement of property disputes. Third parties acted as settlement masters in boundary disputes. In the case of fruit trees, the apple did not fall far from the tree. Fallen fruit was property of the owner of the tree.

Table Eight described remedies for tort damages, regarding theft as a type of tort. In 450 BCE, as it is today, there was compensation as damages for harm, and restitution for criminal acts. Crimes and punishment, as offenses against Rome, were a separate matter.

Damage to a person was compensable by an eye-for-an-eye, or payment in cash or service. Damage to property was compensated by gold or goods. Theft of crops was a capital offense. Sacrificing thieves to the gods in a Forum temple had a deterrent effect on crime.

Table Nine made it clear to all that citizenship was precious and only the Senate could determine who was a citizen or was availed of the rights of citizenship. A Roman citizen would never be extradited to stand judgement or imprisonment by laws of another government. No citizen could be executed for a criminal act without a trial.

Finally, Table Nine was clear that to be effective, judges must be impartial. Bribery of a judge was a crime. The Twelve Tables were silent on bribery of public officials.

The last three tables were brief statements to clarify miscellaneous items. Table Ten restricted women from expressing grief at a funeral in any way that caused self-effacement, such as clawing their face, or loud wailing. Table Eleven required marriage only within class. Slaves did not marry their mistress when the master of the house failed to return from a battle. This did not stop the lady of the house from facilitating slave conquest of the household, and a rise in class. Roman mythology is full of such stories. Table Twelve makes masters responsible for acts of their slaves.

# Roman Forum Venue for the Twelve Tables

The Twelve Tables were established law immediately on posting in the Forum. Placement was profound. The Forum was the venue for everything important in Roman life. Begun as the neutral valley between hills of two rival kings, there was a central market in pre-Roman times. At this place, rival kings capitulated to Romulus, the first Roman king. Forever after, it was acknowledged as an important site for meetings and sacrifices. The Forum held several key temples, meeting places, and official pronouncements. Rome grew around the Forum. The modern Roman Senate sits at one end of the Forum.

The flame of Rome burned on the Forum. The flame represented the hearth of home. Vesta was goddess of that hearth, since before Roman times. Vesta was always a virgin, hence, the Vestal Virgins of Rome. The Roman Senate was located close to the Temple of Vestal Virgins, close to the symbolic hearth of the people.

In the 3rd century CE, Roman Emperor Constantine moved his headquarters to Constantinople, a safe distance from the Senate. Constantine was the first Christian emperor. He was also a collector of statues and building materials, used to decorate his new city and its Hippodrome. Constantine stripped roofing from temples on the Forum. Structures on the Forum decayed from weather and disuse. Churches replaced temples. New laws, or restatement of Roman law, issued from the eastern capital of the realm.

# SPORTS – CONSTANTINOPLE /ISTANBUL

## Nika Riot, Corpus Juris and Hagia Sophia

*Hagia Sophia*

For many resplendent reasons, Istanbul is a popular cruise ship port on any itinerary that includes ports of the Black Sea, or Eastern Mediterranean. This city of over fifteen million is the fifth largest city in the world by population. It sits in Asia and Europe. Notable for cruise travelers, a short walk from the dock are famous buildings, familiar sites from storybooks and travel catalogs, more amazing when experienced in person.

The greatness of Istanbul is the product of four forces of the 3rd to 15th centuries. Constantine the Great, Serbian born, Roman general, expanded the Greek world conquered by Alexander the Great six centuries before, and the Roman city of Byzantium, making it his new capital, Constantinople. Old roads led to Rome. From 330 CE, the hub of the world by land and sea was Constantine's capital city. Constantine was the first Christian emperor, so he built the first Christian churches, including Hagia Sophia.

By the 6th century, power of the Roman Empire waned. Constantine's city was shabby and his Hagia Sophia needed repair. Enter Justinian I and his empress Theodora in 527. Together the power couple rebuilt the city and reconquered the empire by 534. Justinian fostered three law schools, where he decreed teaching Corpus Juris Civilus, the Law of Justinian. Justinian's laws incorporated Christianity with civility.

While Justinian waged battle across the empire, Theodora was a force in the capital. Her support for a sports team began the Nika Riot of 532, in which much of the city burned, including Hagia Sophia. That politics, religion, and sports are topics left off the table in polite conversation began with the Nika Riots. Penance for Justinian was rebuilding Hagia Sophia to majestic heights, reestablishing the proud capital of Constantine.

The fourth defining force came in 1453, when Ottoman Turks conquered Constantinople and made it Istanbul, the capital of the Muslim, Ottoman Empire. Hagia Sophia became a mosque. Just as Constantine desired building churches unlike pagan temples, the Ottoman challenge was creating mosques unique to churches. To their credit, Hagia Sophia as a mosque preserved Justinian features.

Today Istanbul preserves the legacy of Justinian in the Hagia Sophia, and the Code of Justinian survives in cannon law. This is a story in the city of Justinian, where he drafted his code of law, rebuilt his church, and proved that politics and sports do not mix.

## *Corpus Juris Civilus* – Justinian Code

Justinian rebuilt the Roman Empire and the capital city, giving him justification for rewriting laws of Roman society. The old laws, the Twelve Tables, were posted in Rome, in the pagan era. The new laws were written in Latin, imbued with Christian ethics.[78]

Over the millennium since the Twelve Tables, continuous interpretation, editing, and amendments resulted in a voluminous, incongruous body of Roman law. Justinian appointed a commission to draft a code superseding all prior code. It was a force of law.

The final issuance of the commission in 534, was *Corpus Juris Civilus*. This code made Christianity the state religion. Pagans were not citizens in Justinian's empire. Thus began the right of a sovereign to determine religion of subjects. Only the sovereign could order execution. Pagan sacrifice was murder, punishable by death of pagan practitioners.

Christian concepts did not provide a system for resolution of secular relationships. Justinian's code filled the void with Institutes of Gaius, a 2nd century jurist. Though Gaius was pagan, his rulings provided precedent of an impartial jurist in areas of property disputes, family matters, and estate succession. These concepts endure in modern law.

## Devine Hagia Sisters: Irene (Peace), Sophia (Wisdom), and Dynamis (Force)

Distinguishing pagan practice from Christian prayer required churches look nothing like Roman temples. Constantine built two Roman temples in his new capital. He recognized forty thousand builders and artisans were not baptized and needed places of worship.

---

[78] Justinian inherited a labor population of Greeks. The code was translated into Greek in the next century.

The church built by Constantine in 337, was wood and stone. Since Constantine was the first Christian emperor, there were no models of what a church should look like. Jesus preached in Synagogues. His apostles preached on steps of pagan temples. Constantine kept the idea of a congregation, facing the priest, who stood at the altar.

For the architectural concept of a church, Constantine looked to democratic Roman basilicas. A basilica was a meeting hall, the venue for the commodities exchange market and law courts. It was an oblong building with a center aisle leading to an apse, a raised area. On the apse were chairs in a semicircle, where speakers discussed matters in the open, for the benefit of those seated or standing along aisles. The bishop's throne was not democratic, nor found in a basilica. It came later when religion developed structure.

In his churches, Constantine wanted a narthex, that is a vestibule, near the entrance, where unbaptized souls were welcome to listen to the word of God. Next to the narthex were vestibules for baptism. Over the next century, churches took the shape of a cross, retaining the center aisle lined with columns. Eastern Orthodox churches have four equal prongs. Roman Catholic churches have a transept leaving three-fourths of the length of the church for the congregation, and beyond the transept is the apse, altar, and chapel.

Since no church doctrine dictated his choices, Constantine dedicated churches to divine virtues of peace, wisdom, and power. Hagia Irene was dedicated to peace, Hagia Sophia to wisdom, and Hagia Dynamis to power. There is no Hagia Dynamis in Istanbul. A church of that name exists in Greece. Whether Constantine built three sanctuaries in Istanbul is unknown. He built numerous monuments in Rome and throughout the empire.[79]

Hagia Irene is the large brick church seen and ignored by tourists as they walk through the garden to the Topkapi Palace. It sits on foundations of the temple of Aphrodite, of wood and stone. It burned in the Nika Riot of 532, and stood repaired in 548, until damaged in an 8th century earthquake. Repaired again, Hagia Irene stands today.

---

[79] For a guide to Rome of Constantine see www.pilgrimstorome.org.uk, last visited January 19, 2015.

Hagia Irene was the central church until completion of the Hagia Sophia. It remained in use until 1453. Ottoman sultans put their palace on the peninsula, leaving Hagia Irene behind a wall. Hagia Irene became a storage depot for arms and treasure. Today perfect acoustics of Hagia Irene make it an ideal venue for classical music concerts.

Constantine placed Hagia Sophia in a premier spot in his new city. Completion of the church in 360 was left to his son Constantine II. The commanding structure that stuns visitors today was the effort of Emperor Justinian, completed in 537, after the first church burned in 415, and the Nika Riot claimed the second structure in 532.

## Sports Fans Riot

The Nika Riot of 532 had nothing to do with pagans versus Christians. The riot was the result of fan rivalry in a sporting event that spilled beyond the arena, encompassing the city. Zealous team rivalry is older than Christianity.

In the spirit of Christianity, Constantine outlawed gladiator games. Instead, chariot races were an emperor-approved sport. People enjoyed watching dangerous sport. They attended races with the same fervor that they brought to man versus beast in the Coliseum. Chariot races were only slightly less deadly than gladiator contests.

Chariot races were in the Hippodrome on a long, narrow, oval track. At the center of the track Constantine placed a row of stone columns and statues collected across the realm. Three remain in place today, on the mall that is the site of the Hippodrome.

As charioteers raced around the track, racers tried driving opponents into stone columns, where they were crushed or injured. Some spectators threw obstacles onto the track, causing racers to swerve in avoidance, and crash into another racer. The crowd did not come to see the winner so much as the survivor. There were no rules, or referees.

In Rome, charioteers were either on the Blue or Green team. Team alliances continued in Constantinople. Historians speculate teams and/or spectators were divided on class, politics, or religious lines. People attended games wearing face-paint of the team color.

People attended games expecting excitement. On the fateful game day in 532, there was additional tension caused by two dozen new taxes, covering costs of a series of successful, but expensive wars. There were earlier riots and Justinian hung the ringleaders. The rope broke sparing two condemned men. One man was a Blue and the other a Green. Crowds cheering racers directed cheers to the emperor. They shouted *Nika, Nika*, which means win, win, or conquer. They wanted the men spared second gallows.

Empress Theodora was a notorious Blue supporter, after Green supporters disparaged her past as a street performer. Emperor Justinian was a Blue supporter, who created a rift with Blues when he instigated new taxes. On game day in 532, Greens were angry the royal family did not show them greater support. Blues were angry for withdrawal of support. Cheers for racers were also taunts directed toward the emperor and tax ministers.

The royal pair sensed the crowd boiling with anger. They left the arena through a private exit. The crowd poured into the street. In anger, they lit fires.

In three days of riots, most of Constantinople was in flames. The crowd demanded termination of the chief tax officer. Emperor Justinian complied. Concession was too late. The crowd was invigorated. They called for a new emperor.

Justinian felt the better part of discretion was pack and quickly leave. Theodora had a cool head. She famously told Justinian that he would regret leaving. She stayed. She saw power in purple; the ability to lead as a royal.

Justinian called his generals. They came in full armor with Goth mercenaries. Soldiers went into the Hippodrome with axes and swords slashing unarmed citizens. By the end of the fifth day all was quiet. An estimated thirty thousand people lay dead in the city of three hundred thousand.

At the time of the riot, Justinian was emperor five years. He continued reigning thirty-three years. Once the riot ended, the tax minister was reinstated. Games continued with fewer, subdued fans.

# Hagia Sophia Reborn

Perhaps Justinian rebuilt Hagia Sophia desiring to overcome stigma of the Nika Riots. He succeeded in building the largest house of prayer for the next millennium.[80] Its golden dome inspired faithful, converts, and visitors, who swore the sun kissed the church lid.

Justinian commissioned Isidore of Miletus and Anthemius of Tralles as church architects. Isidore and Anthemius were mathematicians, not architects. They knew how to measure size of a structure and determine the amount of material needed. The pair knew how to assemble, train, and manage an army of workers. Seen from the Bosporus today, Hagia Sophia is a massive undertaking in brick and plaster.

Justinian retained Constantine's model church, with enlarged proportions. The new dome had a diameter of 101 feet and a height at the center of 160 feet. This dome imploded during an earthquake and required replacement in 562. The final dome soared to 182 feet. Justinian brought green marble from Thessaly, black stone from the Bosporus, and yellow stone from Syria. Columns came from the Temple of Artemis at Ephesus.

Today Hagia Sophia remains one of the greatest surviving examples of Byzantine architecture. If the church resembles the Blue Mosque, it is because the design was an inspiration for great Ottoman buildings. When Justinian first entered the church, even without stunning mosaics that followed, he fell to his knees and cried, *Solomon, I have outdone thee!*[81] He spent 300,000 gold pounds, $400 million today.

The next emperor, Justinian II added decorative mosaics. During the iconoclastic period in Eastern Orthodoxy, from 726 to 843, figurative mosaics were destroyed. Mosaics seen today were created late in the 9th century. Christ, saints, and church fathers are amply represented, as are Justinian and Theodora.

---

[80] The next church competing with Hagia Sophia in size was Seville Cathedral completed in 1520.
[81] Referring to Jerusalem.

Later monarchs Constantine IX and Zoë flank Christ, in gold tile. Mosaics lost in an earthquake in 1894, were replaced with paintings.

When the doge of Venice sacked Constantinople in the 4th Crusade of 1204, relics in the Hagia Sophia were removed. Upon reconquest in 1261, a marker was installed in the rear, second floor of Hagia Sophia, as though marking the tomb of Venetian doge Enrico Dandolo. It was a popular place to stand for personal relief. Locals discretely and humorously paid their respects to the doge. The tomb is symbolic, not actual.

In 1453, Hagia Sophia became Ayasofya Mosque. The new owners were good caretakers. Under the Turkish regime, the building received much-needed repair.

Mosques are devoid of iconography. They contain geometric designs and calligraphy. When occupying Hagia Sophia, the Ottomans covered abundant mosaics with plaster, preserving them. When the church to mosque became a museum, plaster was removed revealing golden mosaics of Constantine, Empress Zöe, and Christ.

Sometime in the 9th or 10th century, Vikings visited Constantinople, as mercenary soldiers in the army of the emperor. A Viking visited Hagia Sophia and recorded his presence in graffiti. Etched in Viking rune is ***Ulf was here.***

Over the 18th and 19th centuries candles were replaced with oil lamps. Sayings of the Prophet Mohamed hung from walls. Justinian would be pleased to see his building, though it is not a church.

# HISTORIC PRESERVATION/ REPATRIATION - EGYPT & SUDAN

## Shabaka's Stone and the Rosetta Stone

*Rosetta Stone in British Museum (credit Hans Hillewaert Creative Commons)*

*Kush Pharaoh Cairo Museum*

As travelers visit historic sites of the world, conspicuous are missing pieces residing miles away in museums and private collections of the world. Over time, in the aftermath of war, or decline of civilizations, bits of tangible culture taken as prizes were removed from original context. Some items, such as stone statues, are icons of past civilizations. Items may be critical pieces in the story of ongoing peoples. Items of seemingly mundane use in ancient times may be imbued with heightened importance given scarcity and historic patina. Removal of burial goods, prized by archaeologists defining remnants of a culture, interrupt repose of ancestors. Human remains of any age or culture are not owned.

Movement of stones, gems, artifacts, and human remains from place of origin to collections raises questions of ownership and control.[82] Possession does not infer ownership. Years of control by absence of claims may not transfer ownership to the possessor. Consider instances where owners, or descendants, are unaware of hidden items, such as Nazi Provenance, that is art taken between 1935 and 1945, still surfacing from long hidden collections. After centuries of colonial domination, African nations gaining independence in final years of the twentieth century are locating and making claims to objects of culture removed from palaces and temples without permission.

Though co-opting culture in material remains is a human rights issue, there is no international court, such as the Hague, offering a venue for resolution of rights. Some nations promulgate self-rule. Claimants bring claims where nations allow, or in the common law, or in the court of public opinion. The result is haphazard repatriation, without effect of precedent, such as the decision of France to repatriate Benin Bronzes to the nation, without regard to whether the bronzes were removed with or without permission and were individually or group owned when removed to France.

Facts surrounding removal, while important, may not be the determining factor. Consider the Klimt painting of Adele Bloch-Bauer, repatriated to the heir as designated by the owner, for years claimed as cultural patrimony and inalienable property of Austria. Facts of lawful ownership and removal during

---

[82] For further exploration, see: Hutt & Blanco, Cultural Property Law, American Bar Association, 2nd ed, 2017.

the Nazi era were never in dispute. The matter resolved when Austria and the claimant agreed to binding arbitration.

Joining the cadre of ongoing disputes are the Shabaka Stone of Sudan and Rosetta Stone of Egypt, both in the British Museum. Stories of the stones provide fascinating examples of the importance of historic preservation to cultures and complex repatriation disputes.

## Shabaka's Stone

*Kalabsha Temple Kingdom of Kush Sudan*

Between 2600 BCE and 300 CE the Upper Nile area was domain of the Kingdom of Kush. Rulers of Kush, competitors to pharaohs of Egypt, conquered Egypt in 744 BCE, becoming the 25$^{th}$ dynasty of pharaohs; the Black pharaohs of the ancient world. Kush is also known through history as Nubia, land of gold, and modern Ethiopia, the land of copper.

The 25$^{th}$ Dynasty of Egyptian pharaohs, the Nubian Dynasty, lasted from 744 to 656 BCE. The kingdom of Kush was at its zenith. Upper and Lower Egypt were reunified for the first time in millennia. Nubian pharaohs, led by Piye, Shebitku, and Shabaka, renewed ancient Egyptian ceremony and traditional practices, effectively energizing an otherwise dying culture. Temples and burial pyramids were built, in the style of great pyramids of the third millennia

BCE, only smaller. Eventually, unified Egypt was conquered by the powerful Assyrian empire, with its army of literal Biblical proportions.

The Black pharaohs of Egypt are little known by name, although their statues fill museums in Cairo, Turin, and New York. Kushite pharaohs were able warriors, who over time repelled Alexander the Great, Romans, and Persians. Kushite pharaohs were queens as often as kings. In the Christian era, Nubians were Christians, holding the line on Arabization west of the Red Sea. Though Nubia was consumed by the Ottoman Empire, Sudan gained independence in 1956.

The greater region of Nubia comprises northern Ethiopia, the Sudan, and southern Egypt, also known as Upper Egypt, where the Nile River, flows north to the Mediterranean. Some of the earliest civilizations of humans lived in this area.

Kush civilization is of Biblical heritage. Kush, or Cush, was a son of Ham and thus a grandson of Noah. His brothers were Put, Canaan and Mizraim. Mizraim is ancient Hebrew for Egypt. Greeks referred to Kush as Aethiopia. Over a millennium of intermarriage of Egyptians and Nubians produced more Black royals than those within the 25th Dynasty. However, it was the century dominance of the Kingdom of Kush, when it controlled Lower Egypt, that marked a kingdom highpoint.

In 744 BCE, Pharoah Piye's army of Kush went north from Napata, Karima in Sudan today, and conquered Egypt. As Pharaoh of a united Egypt, Piye revitalized the capital at Memphis. He renewed building pyramids. Pageantry of ancient Egypt was renewed.

Piye's military victories were accomplished with chariots and a cavalry of fine horses. When he died, several of his horses were embalmed with him. A desire for further conquest was the undoing of Piye. He met defeat in Gaza, attempting control of Israel.

Shebitku completed conquest of Lower Egypt by 706 and took residence in Memphis. Shebitku kept Assyrians at bay. Some accomplishments of Shebitku are attributed to his successor, Shabaka. Shabaka restored holy places, providing employment for temple priests, the ones who wrote history.

The Shabaka Stone, in the British Museum since 1805, is a testament to preservation of Egyptian history by this third Nubian pharaoh. The stone arrived in England in a time of avid interest in deciphering hieroglyphics. British and American Egyptologists determined the stone, ordered by Shabaka, and installed in his capital at Memphis in the 7th century BCE, was an inscription repeating First Dynasty text, from decaying papyrus.

The message on the Shabaka Stone extolls success of pharaohs uniting Upper and Lower Egypt, thirty centuries BCE. Shabaka's two predecessor pharaohs reunited the kingdom. Accomplishments of three millennia past stood with his dynasty. Pageantry and continuity were hallmarks of successful pharaohs.

In later centuries, the Shabaka Stone was used as a millstone, erasing many hieroglyphics. Enough of text remained to credit Shabaka with preserving some of the earliest recorded human thoughts. Nubian pharaohs were placed within lineage of god-rulers of the Nile.

Succeeding Nubian pharaohs restored monuments, including at Karnak, while their armies kept the Assyrian Empire from overwhelming Egypt. Kushian pharaoh Taharqa reigned from 690 to 664 BCE. He succeeded, or usurped, Shabaka. His time is known for abundant food produced from successive Nile floods, which nourished the fields.

Prosperity during Taharqa's reign enabled construction of burial pyramids and temples, several which stand in north Sudan today. When Assyrians conquered Lower Egypt, Taharqa fled to Thebes. In Karnak are a temple and column commemorating Taharqa. In 656 BCE, the 25th Dynasty ended, as pharaohs of Kush returned to Napata.

The final capital of the Kingdom of Kush was at Meroë. Today the city holds a cluster of gates leading to pyramid tombs of pharaohs of Kush, which are a World Heritage Site. Statues of pharaohs of Kush feature prominently. The Shabaka Stone completes the picture of the greatness of a dynasty, little known, its iconic link in a foreign museum.

# Rosetta Stone – Key to Ancient Egypt

The most famous stone is the Rosetta Stone of Egypt, held in the British Museum in London. The museum rates the stone fragment of a priestly decree, as its number one visitor attraction.[83] The stone was created for local appeal. It became an object of desire between French and English academics in internecine warfare for decades. No one can argue the Rosetta Stone is a key to understanding ancient Egypt and the name Rosetta is synonymous with attainment of knowledge. Egypt wants the stone in its museum.

The Rosetta Stone was quarried in Upper Egypt, not far from Aswan Dam, and brought to Memphis, priestly capital of Egypt. In 196 BCE, it was used in a stela, the decorated slab on which messages were created, for posting in temples, in the time of pharaohs. It stood for six centuries, near a statue of its patron pharaoh, until the beginning of the Christian era. Then the temple, the stela, and ancient edifices were left to crumble.

Through the Middle Ages, Egypt became an Arab domicile. Arab scholars pondered the meaning of hieroglyphics on stones around them. Language of hieroglyphics eluded ancient Greek scholars. Homer attempted deciphering hieroglyphics in the 7th century BCE and Greek historian Herodotus tried unlocking meaning in the 5th century BCE.[84]

Late in the 18th century CE, there was heightened excitement over study of ancient language. Ancient Sanskrit of India was translated into English and ancient Phoenician was deciphered. The meaning of hieroglyphics remained unknown, despite several and continuing attempts by British, French, German, American and Arabic scholars to do so.

Napoleon entered Egypt in 1799, with soldiers and scholars, intending world domination of cultures. While reinforcing a centuries-old fort, from which to wage war on Turkish Mamluk rulers of Egypt, supported by British troops, a French engineer, with a keen eye, spotted a stone, used to build the old fort, on which he saw three types of writing. He recognized the stone as special

---

[83] Richard Parkinson, The Rosetta Stone, The British Museum Press, London, 2005.
[84] E. A. Wallis Budge, The Rosetta Stone, US edition 2018.

and shipped it to the French station in Alexandria for study. Thereafter, the Rosetta Stone, named for the town where it was retrieved, became an object of constant study, continuing today.[85]

The Rosetta Stone is less than four feet tall, almost thirty inches wide, a foot thick and weighs one thousand, six hundred and eighty pounds.[86] It is a lower piece of a stela. It holds the message of priests in 196 BCE, proclaiming support from the pharaoh, in gold, temple building, and exemption from taxation for priests, in exchange for military victory, long life for the pharaoh, and prosperity for Egypt.

Rosetta Stone holds a public relations message to unify people behind the pharaoh, in deference to priests. To accomplish this purpose, the message repeats three times on the stela. At the top, under decorative carving, is sacred language of the gods, known only to priests. These are hieroglyphics. Fourteen of twenty-nine lines of writing are preserved.

By the 2nd century, when the Rosetta Stone was carved, business transactions required development of writing, less formal and less time-consuming to record on stone. This Egyptian writing is known as Demotic. Demotic was the language of transactions such as inventories and sales contracts. Non-priests of Egypt communicated in Demotic. On the Rosetta Stone, below hieroglyphics, are thirty-two lines of Demotic script, a complete copy of the message.

Below Demotic script, the message is repeated in ancient Greek. In the 2nd century BCE, Egypt was dominated by Greeks. Greeks revered their own gods, ignoring Egyptian priests. There are fifty-four lines of ancient Greek on the stone, minus a lower corner.[87]

Priests directing creation of the stela wanted everyone to know their message. Several identical stela were created, positioned throughout the land, standing next to statues of the patron pharaoh, Ptolemy V. The number of replications is unknown.

---

[85] Rosetta is near present day Rashid on the Nile Delta Mediterranean coast.
[86] That is, 112.3 centimeters tall, 75.7 wide and 28.4 thick, weighing in at 762 kilograms.
[87] There are spelling mistakes in Greek, indicating temple craftsmen of Memphis knew Demotic and Hieroglyphics, while they were not as experienced in Greek, as were Greek palace officials in Alexandria. Parkinson, at 13.

The message on Rosetta Stone is the Decree of Memphis. A little history explains necessity of such a decree. Egypt was ruled by Egyptian god-pharaohs from ancient times until 332 BCE, when Alexander the Great conquered the Eastern Mediterranean. Alexander was Greek.[88] When he died, Greek generals divided his empire. General Ptolemy took Egypt, where he began Ptolemy dynasty of Egyptian Pharaohs.[89]

Greeks had their own gods. Still, to be a pharaoh meant being divine, which necessitated adopting local cosmology. Ptolemy pharaohs facilitated trade with the Greek world, resulting in Greeks emigrating to Egypt for commercial opportunity. Prosperous Greeks, living in Egypt, pushed locals down the social chain, to menial jobs. When the great Ptolemy capital of Alexandria rose, fortunes of the historic capital Memphis declined. Most disadvantaged by the new power center, were priests of Memphis.

During the reign of Ptolemy IV, from 221 BCE to 205, priests fomented civil strife. When Ptolemy V was six years old, his father died in suspicious circumstances. When Ptolemy V was fourteen, his mother, Arsinoe, died in a deliberately set fire.

By 196 BCE, tempers cooled. Priests in Memphis issued the decree of Ptolemy V, extolling the pharaoh's support for stability of tradition, led by Egyptian priests. Supremacy of Egyptian tradition over Greek was declared in the trilingual message of the stela.

In the Christian era, Egyptians and Greeks became Christian. Temples survived as Christian churches. In 640 CE, control of Egypt shifted during the Arab conquest of Egypt and northern Africa. Islam became dominant. Ancient Egyptian stela were repurposed.

In 1798, Britain and France were again at war. Napoleon entered Egypt intent on breaking the British supply link to India. In Paris, Napoleon founded the Louvre, then sent home cultural conquests from far reaches of his troops. He sought museum treasure in Egypt.

---

[88] Alex was Macedonian. Macedonia is claimed by Greeks as part of Greece. Alex's father was Philip of Macedonia.

[89] Cleopatra, who lived from 69 BCE to 30 BCE, was the first Ptolemy Pharaoh to speak Egyptian.

In 1799, French troops reinforced Ottoman forts in Egypt to defend against English-supported Turks. While strengthening walls of French christened Fort Julian, a soldier noticed a chunk of stone with three types of writing. Always looking for special artifacts, the soldier sent the stone to Alexandria for examination by French scholars.

The stone was immediately recognized by a French general as special. It was believed the tri-lingual inscriptions would unlock secrets of ancient Egypt. The stone was spread with ink and copies were pressed onto paper, for dissemination to scholars at the French *Institut d' Egypte*, and to scholars in England and Germany.

Also in 1799, Admiral Nelson led the British in a naval victory against the French. When British troops arrived to dispossess the French general of Egyptian treasures, he asserted personal ownership of the Rosetta Stone. Britain took the stone as a *spoil of war*, loaded it onto captured French ship, *L' Egyptienne*, and sent the stone to England.

Officials at the British Museum painted the Rosetta Stone with an inscription indicating it was a gift to the museum by King George III. Britain soon withdrew from Egypt, leaving it in 1803, to the Ottoman general Mohammed Ali.[90] The stone was coated in white chalk to facilitate viewing script. Too heavy for installation on the wooden floor of the museum Egyptian gallery, the Rosetta Stone was planted in the sculpture gallery.

For two centuries, the Rosetta Stone sat among treasures of Egypt, dimly lit in the museum and somewhat obscure, without interpretive signage, although well represented on post cards and gift shop memorabilia. In 2004, mounting pressure to return objects of culture to nations of origin, prompted better display of the item Britain regards as its property. The Rosetta Stone sits in a plexiglass case, well-lit and temperature controlled.

---

[90] The British returned to Egypt in 1882, as a colonial overseer.

# Deciphering the Stone – Linguistics and Egyptology

*Champollion Table (public domain)*

So entwined with Egypt is academia in Europe and America, that study of Egypt has its own area of academic inquiry, known as Egyptology. The Rosetta Stone was an instigator of Egyptology when it rose from war booty to icon of inquiry. The man who is credited with deciphering Hieroglyphics on the Rosetta Stone, Jean-François Champollion, was elected in 1831, to the first chair in Egyptology in the world, at Collége de France. Author Amelia Edwards, who achieved financial security with her book, *A Thousand Miles Up the Nile*, endowed the first British chair in Egyptology in 1892.[91] Since the mid-19th century, renown academic institutions offer Egyptology studies.

When the Rosetta Stone left the battlefield in Egypt, it entered the academic battlefield of French and British scholars in Paris and London. Just as Egyptian pharaohs sought immortality in Hieroglyphic praises, academics of Europe knew deciphering ancient language meant immortality in academia. Two leading contenders, one British and the other French, became national champions in the Olympic quest in the field of linguistics.

British contender and early favorite to crack the code of Hieroglyphics, Thomas Young was educated in Edinburgh and Cambridge.[92] Young was a brilliant medical doctor, made significant contributions to knowledge of how the human eye perceives color, and invented a light bulb. He coined the term energy and measured stress on materials. A Quaker, he refused to eat sugar, as a product of the slave trade. In 1814, Young looked for similarities in Greek and Demotic. He progressed on Demotic text not Hieroglyphics.[93]

A major contribution of Young to Egyptology is identifying oval frames as cartouches, containing names of kings. On the Rosetta Stone, Young identified pharaoh Ptolemy V. He worked on Hieroglyphics to his death, identifying an Egyptian numerical system.

The academic prize in Hieroglyphics went to Frenchman Jean-François Champollion. Champollion, seventeen years junior to Young, born into a modest family, was without an ability to see the stone in London, or Egypt.

---

[91] Amelia Edwards was born in 1831 and died in 1892. Her self-illustrated book was released in 1877.
[92] Thomas Young was born in 1773 and died in 1829.
[93] See John Ray, The Rosetta Stone and the Rebirth of Ancient Egypt, Harvard University Press, Cambridge, 2007.

Impoverished much of his short life, Champollion irritated men of academia with his wit, youth, and low social standing.[94]

Champollion's teacher of Chinese, Coptic, and Greek was a friend of Young, who preferred success be won by a Brit. The teacher hampered Champollion where he could and demeaned the younger man's accomplishments, until Champollion overcame all detractors with undeniable results. In 1824, when Champollion presented findings to an international body of scientists, in which Young was the London Royal Society delegate, Young was gracious to acknowledge Champollion earned a place in history of linguistics.

 In 1826, Champollion received a post in the Louvre as curator of the Egyptian collection. He traveled to London to see the Rosetta Stone and to Egypt, to the Temple of Karnak. In 1831, he was elected to hold the first chair in Egyptology at the Collége de France.

Academic duties included entertaining dignitaries and philanthropic supporters. The press of research and publication took a toll on Champollion. He enjoyed food and gained excess weight. In 1832, at age forty-one, he died of a stroke. His brother completed their Grammaire égyptien, relied upon by Egyptology scholars today.

Egyptology scholar John Ray describes how Champollion deciphered Hieroglyphics by noting there are three types of writing, regardless of language.[95] These are: picture, pun, and cartoon. A picture is recognized as an object. A pun is when pictures are combined to create a phrase, such as a bee next to a leaf for – belief. Cartoons are universal, not dependent upon language, such as road hazard signs, or symbols on clothing for care.

Champollion was familiar with pun in Chinese. He looked at Hieroglyphics for pictures, a phonetic value, or part of a phrase. He determined an alphabet, in any language, began from pictures, which evolved to sounds, represented by a letter. Over millennia, pictures drifted from use. In Hieroglyphics, Champollion found symbols could be figurative, symbolic, or phonetic signs, or all three in one word, phrase, or sentence.

---

[94] Champollion irritated Frenchmen with support of Napoleon. Concept of right and left comes from Napoleonic assembly, where supporters and detractors sat to each side of the room and glared at each other.
[95] Ray at 82.

Champollion recognized determinatives. Determinatives end sentences, categorize words, or distinguish meanings in similar signs. For instance, a yoke is the harness of a horse, or the burden of taxation. There is no punctuation in Hieroglyphics.

The Rosetta Stone enabled Champollion to compare Greek to Demotic and discern meaning in Hieroglyphics. The more Champollion resolved, the more he built an understanding of language. Imagine his delight walking through the great columned hall of Karnak, able to read and understand inscriptions on stones.

To speak the name of the dead, is to make them live again.[96] Speaking Hieroglyphics was never the goal, except names of pharaohs. The goal was understanding meaning in words of the Egyptian gods. Thanks to Champollion, meanings are alive again.[97]

The Rosetta Stone sits in the British Museum as a *Spoil of War*. It is an icon of understanding the deep past. It is testament to British dominance in war over France. There is an argument for placing the Rosetta Stone in the Louvre. Champollion was a curator at the Louvre and the stone was located and brought to prominence by a French officer. The Rosetta Stone made a brief visit to the Louvre in the 1970s.

The Rosetta Stone remains an object in controversy over control of culture. The British Museum raises the same arguments made to justify retaining the Parthenon Marbles. Paternal arguments of better care and access to visitors is overcome by the new Cairo Museum. That Britain defeated France in a war, in which Egypt was a host not by invitation, does not give rise to arcane concepts of spoils of war, in a domestic object.

---

[96] Ray, at 90.
[97] Champollion translated *The Voyage of Wenamun*, written in 1100 BCE, a story of a mission to Lebanon for wood to build a barge for the god Amun. Travelers have a series of adventures, encounter pirates, and take a detour to Cyprus, where they land at the palace of a Queen, centuries prior to Homer and the *Odyssey*. A tale of *The Man Who Was Tired of Life*, in which a man has a conversation with his soul, was not a big seller in ancient Egypt. More popular was a story of young women who enter a wet toga contest.

From an odd bit of booty that arose in a conflict, through conflicts in academia to use its content, the Rosetta Stone is an icon of cross-cultural understanding. It was the key utilized to capture lost knowledge. The Rosetta Stone tells the world that through the written word, culture can endure.

# CIVIC ADMINISTRATION
## - INDIA AND CHINA
### CONFUCIUS AND THE *ARTHASASTRA*

*Hindu Temple India (Feast Studios Elizabeth Herrgott)*

Laws governing civic administration, the operation of localities, and statecraft began well before bands of people identified with city-states, such as Athens and Rome, or nation-states of the 18th to 20th centuries. Confucius, the 5th century BCE Chinese sage, organized moral society and civic administration. Confucianism is not a religion. It is the way of a well-ordered life. In the 2nd century BCE, the *Book of Arthasastra* directed lessons of governance, practical and obligatory.

The depth of Indian culture, and its colorful history, are well known through books from the 2nd century BCE, when India was the center of the world. Lessons from the book of *Arthasastra* taught statecraft at a time when Greek classical scholars and Chinese embassies consulted Indian sultans. It was written in Sanskrit, the root language of eastern societies. Lessons are relevant today.

Confucius commented on 5th century society needing reminders of civilized ways of life. He did not create rules, so much as stated proverbs, repeated as sayings of Confucius. His word became law, in a society where adherence to tradition provided stability.

This review of lessons of the 5th and 2nd centuries BCE remind all that a goal of good governance is universal and timeless. Most remarkable is the extent to which western society values ancient, eastern principles. Confucius might say commonality is peaceful.

## Lessons from the Book of *Arthasastra*

Sanskrit, the language of Hindu, is one of the oldest languages in the world. Its history in India goes back three thousand five hundred years.[98] It is the root language of people across northern India, stopping short of the southern

---

[98] Vedic Sanskrit, the Indo-Iranian language dates to 1500 BCE. By comparison, Mycenaean Greek dates to 1450 BCE and Ancient Greek 750 BCE. Another ancient language, Hittite dates from 1750 BCE. Note: BCE, before current era or CE, current era is the notation used in CTH. Homer wrote the Iliad and the Odyssey in 750 BCE.

peninsula. Tamil is the language of the south. Seventy million Tamil speakers have a language tracible two thousand years.

Hindu sages wrote books in Sanskrit, containing wisdom of the ages. Insight to laws of early society and good governance practiced by early rulers of India is found in the *Arthasastra*. The book was compiled over five centuries, from 2nd century BCE to 3rd century CE, by Hindu scholars, the Braham. The book was followed assiduously by rulers, until lost in the 12th century, when Mongols from the north arrived, with their rules.

An *Arthasastra* was discovered in 1905, and translated in 1915, enabling a picture of the past. Rudrapatna Shamasastry[99] was a Sanskrit scholar and librarian at the Oriental Research Institute in Mysore, India, a repository of ancient texts. Among books he was cataloging was an *Arthasastra*. He translated text, subject to study ever since.

In a Hindu creation story, Manu, the first man, survived a great flood aided by a fish. Manu previously protected the fish, so when the flood came, the fish returned the good gesture. The root of all happiness is in the good gesture, the so-called dharma. In the sutras, sections of Sanskrit books, the root of dharma is Artha, that is right governance, inner-restraint, humility, and serving the aged. Sastra is the Sanskrit word for rules or science. Science is organized knowledge. The *Arthasastra* is the foundation of political science as it was practiced from the 2nd century BCE.

*Arthasastra* is composed of fifteen books, which direct organization of government, with the Raja as king, activities of a king, and the means of war led by the king. Peace is always the preferred option. When necessary, there are open, covert, and silent wars. There are rules in the *Arthasastra* for spying and covert operations.

Included among the sutras is a section on justice. A king is told that loyalty of the people to the king is earned by being just. Kings must be impartial and stand in judgement of enemies as they would a son.

---

[99] He was born in 1868 and lived to 1944.

Kings are advised to keep a council of knowledgeable ministers of integrity. Kings must avoid violence. Initiation of violence, in acts or words, results in disaffection of the people. Failure to punish wrongdoers, as well as wrongful punishment, is to be avoided. Economic crimes of traders, such as conspiracy, are dealt with more harshly in *Arthasastra* than individual crimes, as conspiracy harms well-being of the people.

Marriage laws in *Arthasastra* allow a woman to marry whomever she wishes, if she forgoes dowry, and to remarry if she has been abandoned more than three months. Environmental laws require protecting forests and using state funds to feed horses and elephants too old to obtain food. There are rules in *Arthasastra* for private enterprise, which is encouraged, regulated, and taxed.

Armies of Alexander the Great made a big impact on people of the world. When he died in 323 BCE, his generals divided most of his domain. A leadership void in India was filled by the Mauryas, a Hindu dynasty of rajas. Their code of law was *Arthasastra*.

Mauryas kingdom, reigning from after the death of Alexander to 180 BCE, ruled eighty percent of the land mass of India at its height. The unifying feat was not repeated for more than a millennium. The Mauryas king responsible for uniting India was Asoka, ruling from 297 to 232 BCE, a century after Alexander died. Asoka considered Alexander as his mentor.[100]

Asoka's accomplishments are known as he left messages carved in stone throughout India. Most informative is Asoka Pillar, near Agra. The capital of the pillar, with lions, symbol of the raj, is the national symbol of India today.[101] Asoka tells readers they should fear him as he slew one hundred thousand enemies in war. Buddhism brought him to understand the virtue of peace. He sent his son, Mahinda, to Sri Lanka bringing the word of the Buddha. He then sent maidens, providing nobles of the island Indian wives.

Little is known about dynasties following Mauryas, which ruled for one or two centuries, over fractions of the land, until Guptas ruled from 300 to 500 CE. Known as Golden Guptas for obvious enjoyment of gold and for the age

---

[100] The king is sometimes spelled as Ahsoka. Spelling differs among scholars depending on translations.
[101] See generally, John Keay, India: A History, Grove Press, New York, 2010, at 94.

of poetry and crafts, regulated in quality by guilds, exemplifying their culture. Guptas revived Sanskrit as poetry.[102]

The Gupta raj were poets not warriors. When Huns attacked in 530 CE, their dynasty folded. Arabs came into India as warriors in the 8th century. Arab traders were part of Indian Ocean commerce since the 2nd century. At the millennium, the Cholas kingdom rose in eastern India. Known for fanciful temples, the dynasty was short lived, preferring war, which exhausted resources and royals.

While Cholas rajas were waging war, other rajas developed settled kingdoms, with defined territory, and stable organizations. Several kingdoms were centered on Delhi. Unfortunately, for their continued development, these rajas were inward focused, missing a cataclysmic event happening in their hills. They failed to consult Book VIII of *Arthasastra* on preparation for calamity. It advises unity and forts.

In 1192, Mongols from the north attacked a few rajas. The next year Mongols returned and faced a united group of raj armies, in the Battle of Chandawar. It was the most decisive battle in the history of India. Mohammed of Ghor, a Turkic leader, defeated assembled raj and took Delhi. A new era of India began. The *Arthasastra* was lost for centuries.

## Lessons from Confucius

The time of Confucius is known as the Warring States period in China. Warlords captured turf, receiving taxes from farmers, much like Medieval Europe a thousand years later. Control was transitory. Disruption of lives was bad for farmers, leading to famine.

Kong Qiu, or in deference, Master Kong, in historic reflection known as Confucius, was a minor Chinese court official to the emperor, living from 551 to 479 BCE. Confucius was philosophical, looking back to calmer days of his grandparents. He saw veneration of the ancients as a means of stabilizing

---

[102] Sanskrit Love Poetry is a high art form.

society. Family was his societal core. Respect for others began within the family unit. Confucius is credited with the Golden Rule of respect: Do unto others as you want for yourself, or do not do to others, what you would not want done to you. Confucius suffered a lifetime of derision from jealous courtiers.

In China's history of warring bands, conquering the landscape becoming dynasties of great power, the greatest enemies were internal. As Confucius said of China, when it is apart, it must come together, and when it is together, it must come apart. The wisdom of his words was repeatedly proven in China's history.

Confucius is credited for books of lessons, standards for organizing home and public life. More likely, his sayings were written over time and collected in books, with edits and additions. Confucius did not stand alone in voicing opinions. His was an era of A Hundred Schools of Thought, four centuries in which philosophers fought for ideological recognition, just as warlords fought for physical turf.

At the end of the 2nd century BCE, Qin dynasty emperors imposed their law as the sole authority. It was a short-lived dynasty. The next dynasty was the strong Imperial Han, a dynasty that tied success to strict adherence to Confucius.

The first Han emperor united most of China by 90 BCE, including Manchuria, northern Korea, and west toward the Caspian Sea south of Tibet. Confucius advised emperors to lead rituals not armies. The advice was well taken by Han. Han emperors built tombs to the ancestors. Royals were buried in full body jade suits. A short-term usurper unseated complacent Han. From 618 to 907 CE, Tang dynasty emperors ruled China.

There were five imperial dynasties in China from Han in the 2nd century BCE, to Qing dynasty in 1912. Throughout, Chinese society was structured on dictates of Confucius. In an ethical code of interaction in a just society, Confucius ordered society by function.

At the top of the ladder in society were rulers, then peasants. Peasants were important as they farmed and produced rice, the staple of life, the source of tax to the king. The success of early China was in its ability to feed a large population. Armies capable of conquering territory and resisting conquest from the outside, such as from Japan, were dependent upon large populations of well-fed warriors.

Next rung on the ladder were craftsmen and at the bottom of society were merchants. Merchants were of the lowest level as they contributed nothing to society. Confucius was a courtier. Merchants siphoned off goods meant for the king. Until kings learned to tax goods in commerce, merchants were of no use to royals. Merchants traveled across domains, exhibiting no loyalty to any ruler. In China they were regarded as dangerous.

Japan sent monks to China to learn rules of Confucian ethical society. Between warring giants, Korea's growing population, well supplied with rice, built an independent civilian government. Its small military defended borders, while resources focused on agriculture and artistic culture. Highly informed by Confucius, Korean society was also structured.

Protocol was a religion in China, as British envoy to China William, the Ninth Lord Napier discovered in 1834. Knowing nothing of Chinese protocol or rules of Confucius proved fatal for Napier. Instead of petitioning the viceroy for a meeting to discuss the possibility of a British trade station in Hong Kong, Napier went directly to Canton and demanded an audience with the viceroy. Chinese were in shock at the offense. Foreigners were not to just arrive and travel in China. There were rules. Napier was left in the cold finding his own way back to the British compound. In transit he became ill, suffered from fever in Macau, and never recovered.

Confucius receives cult adoration in modern society, China and beyond, for promoting moral behavior and responsible governance. Consider the circumstances prompting his thoughts. Some timeless lessons of Confucius include:

- When it is obvious goals cannot be reached, do not adjust goals; adjust action steps.
- Practice five virtues of gravity, generosity of soul, sincerity, earnestness, and kindness.
- Real knowledge is to know the extent of one's ignorance.
- Study the past if you would define the future.
- Universally recognized moral qualities are wisdom, compassion, and courage.

- Life is simple, we make it complicated.
- Without feelings of respect men are not distinguished from beasts.
- Bad things are easy to acquire, good is difficult. It is easy to hate and difficult to love.
- Everything has beauty, but not everyone sees it.
- Wherever you go, go with all your heart.

# INDEX

## A

Adomnán, 46, 49
Ally, Pierre d', 112
Arnarson, Ingólfr, 27-28, 35
*Arthasastra,* 169-173

## B

Banks, banking, 20-21, 28, 58, 95, 100-101, 127-128
**Battles**
    Bannockburn (1314), 47
    Carham (1034), 55
    Chandawar (1193), 173
    Cúl Dreimhne (560), 45
    Hastings (1066), 64
    Orlygsstadir (1238), 31
    Plassy (1757), 103
Bayeux Tapestry, 64-65
**Books (Illuminated)**
    Cathach of St. Columba, 45
    Durrow, 47
    Kells, 37, 41, 43, 45-47, 50

## C

Cabot, John, 113
Cabot, Sebastian, 113
Centurione (Bank St. George), 131-132
Champollion, Jean-François, 164
Christian I (Denmark), 18, 20, 30, 32
Clusius, Carolus (L'Escluse), 91
Colbert, Jean Baptiste, 97
Columbus, Christopher, 106-107, 109-110, 128, 132
Confucius, 169-170, 173-175
Córdoba, Francisco Hernandez, 125

## D

Dampier, William, 126
Dávila, Gil Gonzáles, 125
Dávila, Pedrarias, the Cruel, 125
Decree of Memphis (196 BCE), 161
Diaz, Bartholomew, 116
Domesday Book, 61-63, 66
Doria, Andrea, 129-130
Duncan (Scotland), 51, 56-60
Dupleix, Joseph Francois, 102

## E

**East India Company**
    British, 9, 99
    Dutch, 9, 83-85, 96, 99
    French, 9, 96-97, 99-101, 103-104
Edwards, Amelia, 164
Erickson, Leif, 34-35

## F

Fieschi Conspiracy, 130
Fieschi, Gian Luigi, 130

## H

Hanseatic League, 69-70, 72, 74-75
**Historic Sites**
    Iona Abbey, 46, 49, 51-52
    Jarlshof, 15-16, 20, 22-24
    Lindisfarne, 47, 50
    Ring of Brodgar, 15, 21

Rochester Castle, 66-67
Skara Brae, 15-17, 20-22, 24
St. Magnus Cathedral, 19, 23-24
Standing Stones of Stenness, 15, 21
Thingvellir (Iceland), 25-26, 28-29, 33-35
Winchester Law Court, 61, 66
Holinshed, Ralph
*Chronicles of England*, 59

K

Kalmar Union, 16, 19-20, 32
**Kings, Queens, & Royals**
Albert (Sweden), 72
Alexander III (Scotland), 19
Alexander the Great, 146, 157, 161, 172
Asoka (India), 172
Canute (Norway, England), 18, 55
Charles II (England), 87
Constantine (Rome), 144, 146-149, 152
Elizabeth I (England), 54, 59, 74
Ferdinand (Spain), 113-115
Frederick II (HRE), 130
Henry the Lion (Germany), 71
Henry VII (England), 113
Henry, Prince (Portugal), 109, 113
Håkon (Norway), 18, 31, 72
Isabella (Spain), 39
James I (England) VI (Scotland), 58-60
James III (Scotland), 20, 23
João II (Portugal), 113
Justinian (Roman Empire), 146, 150-152
Kenneth (Scotland), 55
Louis XIV (France), 96-98, 101
Louis XVI (France), 96, 103
Macbeth (Scotland), 51-60
Magnus (Norway), 18-19, 23-24, 31-32, 56

Malcolm II (Scotland), 55, 60
Malcolm III (Scotland), 57, 59
Margaret (Norway), 19
Mauryas (India Dynasty), 172
Olaf I (Norway), 18
Olaf II (Norway), 18
Otto (HRE), 78
Philip II (Spain), 84
Piye (Kush/Egypt), 156
Ptolemy V (Egypt), 160-161, 164
Shabaka (Kush/Egypt), 156-158
Shebitku (Kush/Egypt), 156-157
Suleiman Magnificent (Ottoman), 90
Thorvaldsson, Gizur (Iceland), 31
William I (England), 19, 62
William of Orange, 85

L

**Law Codes**
Arthasastra (civic admin), 169-173
Indies (Zoning), 119-122, 124-126
Innocents (War), 49
Justinian (Ethics), 146-147
*Corpus Juris Civilus*, 141, 146-147
*Institutes of Gaius*, 147
Lübeck (Trade), 69, 72, 75
Macbeth (Civil), 53
Schwabenspiegel (Land Title), 77, 79, 81-82
Twelve Tables (Rome Civil), 141-144, 147
Law, John, 95, 100, 102
Louis XV (France), 101

M

Magnusson, Skuli, 33
Mississippi Company (French), 101
Moniz, Dona Filipa, 109
Morgan, Henry, 125
**Museums**
British Museum (London), 156, 158-159, 162, 166

Glamis Castle (Scotland), 54, 57, 60
Hagia Sophia (Istanbul), 141, 145-146, 148-149, 151-152
Iona Abbey, 46, 49, 51-52
Louvre (Paris), 161, 165-166
Skaill House (Orkney), 24

## N

Napier, William, 9th Lord, 175
Nelson, Admiral Horatio, 126
**Norse Sagas**
    Book of Settlements, 27
    Grey Goose (Grágás), 29
    Icelandic Sagas, 27, 34
    Orkney Saga, 18
    Sturlunga Saga, 27

## O

Odo (Bishop & Earl), 65

## P

**People of the Itinerary**
    Anglo, 17
    Cholas, 173
    Gabrieleño, 122
    Guptas (dynasty), 172-173
    Han, 174
    Mauryas (dynasty), 172
    Miskito, 125-126
    Mongols, 171, 173
    Nahuatl, 124
    Normans, 62, 64
    Norse, 16-19, 22, 25-27, 29-32, 34
    Oscan, 135
    Picts, 17-18, 45-46, 51, 54-55
    Qin (dynasty), 174
    Samite, 135
    Saxon, 50, 57, 73, 77
    Tang, 174
Perestrelo, Bartholomew, 109

Perpetuities, Rule, 79
Pliny the Elder, 111
Pliny the Younger, 137-138
Plutarch, 111
**Popes**
    Adrian V, 130
    Alexander VI, 115
    Innocent IV, 130
    Pius II, 112
Ptolemy, 111, 160-161, 164

## R

Rembrandt van Rijn, 92
Repgow, Eike von, 82

## S

**Saints**
    Bracelli, Virginia Centurione, 128
    Columba, 41-47, 49-52
    Finnian, 40, 44-45
    Magnus, 18-19, 23-24, 31-32, 56
    Olaf, 18
    Oran, 46, 48-50
    Paul, Apostle, 135
Sanskrit, 159, 170-171, 173
Scott, Sir Walter
    *The Pirate* 1822, 73
Shabaka
    Shabaka's Stone, 153, 156
Shakespeare, William, 53, 58
Shamasastry, Rudrapatna, 171
Somerled, Roland, 51
Störtebeker, Klaus, 73
Strabo, 112
Sturluson, Snorri, 31
Stuyvesant, Peter, 87

## T

*Táin bó Cuailnge*, 37
Things, Althings, 32

Thule, 16-17
Toscanelli, Paolo, 112
Toypurina, 122
**Treaties**
    Guadalupe Hidalgo (1848), 122
    Rostock (1283), 75
    Stralsund (1370), 72
    Tordesillas (1493), 155
    Utrecht (1572), 85

V

Victual Brothers, 72-73
Vikings, 16, 18, 22, 25-26, 28, 30, 50-51, 55, 57, 71, 106, 152
Von Olmen, Ferdinand, 113

W

Webber, Karl, 138
**World Heritage Sites**
    Amsterdam Canal Rings, 89
    Brodgar Ring (Orkney), 15, 21
    Chiavari (Italy - nominated), 130-131
    Genoa Strade Nuove, 1
        Via Garibaldi, 132
        Palazzo Doria-Spinola, 128, 129
    Hagia Sophia (Istanbul), 141, 145-146, 148-149, 151-152
    Herculaneum (Italy), 134
    Kushite Temples of Napatan, 157-158
    León Cathedral, 119
    Lübeck Hanseatic City, 71
    Newgrange (Ireland), 15
    Roman Forum, 140, 144
    Schwerin Castle (Germany-tentative), 76
    Seville Cathedral, 117, 151
    Skara Brae (Orkney), 15, 20-21
    Standing Stones of Stenness (Orkney), 15, 21
    Thingvellir National Park (Iceland), 34-35

Y

Young, Thomas, 164

www.ingramcontent.com/pod-product-compliance
Lightning Source LLC
Chambersburg PA
CBHW081744100526
44592CB00015B/2298